GW00889927

anchorbooks

Edited
Vivien Linton

To Pause
A While . . .

First published in Great Britain in 2009 by:
Anchor Books
Remus House
Coltsfoot Drive
Peterborough
PE2 9JX
Telephone: 01733 898104
Website: www.forwardpress.co.uk

All Rights Reserved
Book Design by Tim Christian
© Copyright Contributors 2009
SB ISBN 978-1-84418-489-7

Foreword

Anchor Books was established in 1992, with the aim of promoting readable poetry to as wide an audience as possible.

We want to establish an outlet for writers of poetry who may have struggled to see their work in print.

The poems presented here have been selected from many entries, and as always editing proved to be a difficult task.

I trust this selection will delight and please the authors and all those who enjoy reading poetry.

Editor

Vivien Linton

Contents

John Collinson 1

Billy Knox 4

J Allan 4

Elizabeth Hassall 5

Linda Robertson 5

Jacqueline Longley 7

Rosie Oakes 9

Christine Nolan 9

Eddie Jepson 11

G K Raynes 11

John Bliven Morin 13

Amitabh Kumar 13

Tom Ritchie 15

Theresa Hartley-Mace 15

Karen Holm 17

Sandy Baudrey 17

Barbara C Perkins 19

Jay Berkowitz 19

Joyce Hefti-Whitney 21

Elizabeth Scott 21

Trudy Shepherd 23

Barbara Fuller 23

Bonnie Austin 25

Christine Corby 25

Leonard Jeffries 27

E Hogg 27

Raymond Uyok 28

Amanda Hyatt 29

Phil Saunders 30

Diana Price 31

B W Ballard 32

M C Thomas 33

D A Reddish 34

Deborah Harvey 35

George McAdam 36

Sarah Dawes 37

Terry Daley 38

Margaret Montgomery 39

Daniel Woodgate 40

Philip G Clark 41

Carolyn Jones 42

Judy Rochester 43

Colleen Biggins 44

Steven Ilchev 45

Nicholas Hall 46

Margaret Nixon 47

Ann Hathaway 48

Daffni Percival 49

Dianne Audrey Daniels 50

Gregor Cook 51

Audrey Howden 52

Christopher Leith 53

James Robert Proudlove 54

Sheila Bates 55

Karl Delaney 56

S A Brown 57

Anne-Marie Howard 58

Judy Studd 59

N D Hawas 60

Jonathan Hobdell 61

Alan Millard 62

Tom Roach 63

John Walker 64

Ronald Martin 65

B Wharmby 65

Barbara Jermyn 66

Christopher G Elliott 66

Lorna Cameron 67

Rob Barratt 68

Shaun McEwan 69

Josie Pepper 70

Irene Greenall 71

June Melbourn 72

Edith Bright-Butler 73

Stacey Mayer 74

Denis Martindale 75

Mark Andrew Bennett 76

Ellen Spiring 77

Carole Spreddie 77

Martin Winbolt-Lewis 78

Lisa Mills 79

Mark Andrew Bennett 80

Chloe Rose (12) 81
Michael McNulty 82
Dat Guy Dere.. 83
Mark Musgrave.. 83
Chris Creedon 84
Mark Russell... 85
David Charles.. 86
Sean Conway 86
Daz Smith... 87
Shilla Mutamba.. 87
John W Fenn 88
Wendy Andrews-Nevard........................... 89
Barbara Goode 90
P E Woodley.. 91
J Harrington.. 92
Christa Todd 92
John Foster... 93
Karen Logan 93
Brian Hurll... 94
Rosemary Benzing 94
B G Clarke 95
Mike Hynde... 95
Ross Baker.. 96
Greeny62.. 96
Rosemary Jennings.................................. 97
Keith Murdoch 97
Albert E Bird 98
Mary Hughes 98
Simon Foderingham 99
Amanda Beeby 99
Jade Bradley.. 100
Derek Haskett-Jones............................... 101
F L Brain 102
Stella Mortazavi 103
Myra Ranger 104
Philip Mee 105
P Penfold 106
Sid 'de' Knees 107
John Willmott 108
Shirley Thompson 109
Carol Elsmore...110
Ronnie Shaw 111
Lynn Elizabeth Noone 112
Charles Keeble 113
George Bremner.......................................114

Debra Webb 115
Eileen Wilby..115
B Page..116
Avishek Parui...117
Caroline Foster..117
Alister Wilson..118
Katrina M Anderson 118
Denise Castellani......................................119
Bobby Rainsbury 119
D M Walford.. 120
Victorine Lejeune-Stubbs 121
Chris Norton 121
Ian Pulford 122
S Davies 122
J L Rimmer 123
Catherine Blackett 123
James Ayrey 124
Samantha Carroll................................... 125
Beth Stewart 126
D Caomhanach...................................... 127
Edward Spiers 128
Angela Rose Elizabeth Davis 128
Catherine Wigglesworth 129
Neil Turner 129
Philip Hutson 130
Lindsey Nicole Hazle.............................. 130
Carolie Cole Pemberton 131
Betty Bukall... 131
Robert Shorey 132
Susan Roffey 132
Ronald Rodger Caseby 133
E Riggott... 133
Nikky Braithwaite 134
Francis Page 135
Pauline Smithson.................................... 135
Simone Fontana 136
Matthew R Wright 136
Mark VanWarmer................................... 137
Dean Howells 137
Cecilia Moldovan 138
M Sam Dixon 138
Jean Paisley 139
Kimberly Harries.................................... 139
Andy Powell... 140
Julie Brown 140

Donna Salisbury 141
Debbie Legall....................................... 142
Florrie MacGruer 142
Annabelle Tipper.................................. 143
Frances Coast 143
Joan Corneby 144
E L Hannan.. 144
Sandy Fryer... 145
John Shanahan 145
Dorothy M Mitchell............................... 146
Joe Riley.. 146
Len Peach 147
Brian J Meehan 147
Natasha Bowerman 148
S Mullinger.. 148
Simon Wilkins 149
Gareth Culshaw................................... 150
Godfrey Dodds 150
Matthew Griffin 151
Ray Varley 151
Errol Kavan.. 152
Geoff Ward 152
Don Antcliff 153
Steve Hurley.. 153
Gaelyn Joliffe...................................... 154
John Cook 155
Peter Mahoney 155
John Morrison...................................... 156
Shane Telford 156
Ann Beard.. 157
Jean Hendrie 158
Pauline Uprichard 158
Peter Muirhead 159
Heather Campion 159
Colin Burnell 160
Gilberto Dias....................................... 160
Joy Sheridan.. 161
Milly Holme 161
B Williams.. 162
Marion Lee... 162
Fine Buliciri 163
C O Schou 163
Isaac Smith.. 164
David Walmsley.................................... 164
Nicholas Taylor 165

Stuart Pickup 166
Jan Garrod... 166
Maureen Westwood O'Hara 167
Patrick Glasson 167
Keith Miller... 168
Jessica Maxwell-Muller........................ 168
Doris Moore 169
Clinton Cox 169
Margaret Toft 171
Morag Grierson.................................... 171
Avis Scott... 172
Tove Selseth 173

The Poems

Charlbury

No longer is there a stockade,
Which once for the 'churls' was made,
To keep them locked within at night,
But now there is an open site.

Words may change but seldom die,
And there are two that strike my eye,
What's now Stockade they then called Bury,
Add the churl and we have Charlbury.

Today a couple on their feet
Amble slowly down the street,
Pop aside for a bite of grub:
Then the paper, then the pub.

But no one thought this an odd world
When a Porsche stopped, and the door unfurled.
Then a posh man, looking swell,
Walked languidly, into The Bell.

You see, this is now everyone's town,
Be they in jeans, or wearing a gown.
Charlbury is yours, mine, and ours,
See if you can find any prettier flowers!

The sun glitters down its rays
On the Farmers' Open Market days,
Where products are in England born,
Not sweated over from a Chinese dawn.

A drifting cloud in the sky
Was about to rain as it passed by,
But it saw the spread of nature's food,
Then drifted on, and changed its mood.

The cricket club increases sales
Almost as often as it loses bails,
But it's the social pulse that brings members in:
Increased, of course, by the strength of gin.

Ah well! I'd better see to myself,
That's if anything is left on the shelf.
Tread you all now the streets and see,
Walk in your freedom, for we now are all free.

John Collinson

I Am One

I am insane
Unlike any other
I am profane
Drinking life from your mother.
I am a long story
Impossible to cut short
I am your glory
And a dream of a thought.
I am press play
You can't switch me off
I am today
And today is not soft.
I am a scratch
A weed that will grow
I am a match
Impossible to follow.
I am a phase
Of a book made by God
I am this craze
A vicious, dirty dog.
I am not laughing
An invention by Man
I am departing
Like breeze from a fan.
I am a parachute
Falling dangerously
I am the flute
Playing so musically.
I am a seductive
Mess of a hand
I am destructive
Of all who are bland.
I am a whisper
Of secrets unknown
I am a vista
You cannot condone.
I am Aquarius
Ripple in water
I am continuous

Like lust for your daughter.
I am a man
Of this I'm ashamed
I am left hand
I cannot complain.
I am entirety
This is forever
I am respiring
You should know better.
I am a soul
Determined to immortality
I am not scared
Death is normality.
I am a track
Of a train off the rails
I am pseudo
No one we shall hail.
I am similarity
Contradictory to previous
I am always changing
I know this is devious.
I am an eyelid
That shuts to block life
I am of no wing
Rejecting to fight.
I am fixated
In an unstoppable stare
I am degraded
No one really cares.
I am future saint
But no - not expectant
I am so faint
What I said was mistaken.
I am ink
Expelled from this pen
I am trying to think
But now was back then.
I am 24th
Of 1st '94
I am albeit north
South makes me contort.

I am soon
Because time is ticking
I am her womb
I like how that's clicking.
I am penultimate
To ultimate tyrant
I am incompetent
This was your moment.
I am Haphein
Notarna
Saleyn
I am collapsing
Number one is now slain.

Billy Knox

Always And Forever

Life is such a crazy path,
It twists you left and right,
I guess I need you here with me
To get me through the night.
Why did you leave me here alone?
You know I need you here.
Just to know you're by my side,
To conquer all my fear.
Life goes on, I always say,
You get over all the pain,
But just remember me and you,
And why it's not the same.
We'll never have another chance
To salvage right from wrong,
There always is another place,
But that road is just too long.
And as we go our separate ways,
I wish we were together,
But don't forget that I love you,
Always and . . . forever.

J Allan

4

Untitled

When I am a picture, a memory on cardboard
and you must dust me daily,
What will you see?
Black and white coldness, a rather weary person,
or the loving that I had for you, with all the heart of me?
When I am a picture and perhaps you won't remember
as sure you will forget a bit, as sure we all must do,
Try and think of all the laughter and the fun we had together,
A bit of old life's memory that is living on in you.

Elizabeth Hassall
With Love and Memories

Untitled

Grey skies
drizzle and rain.
Bare branches on
the trees again.
In the mornings
fog and mist
in the air
leaves twirl and twist.
Cold winds
dark nights
summer flowers
out of sight.
Hats and scarves
for chilly walks,
fireworks, sparklers
bonfire, Guy Fawkes
November.

Linda Robertson
x

The Kind Miracle

They came from different backgrounds
The match was thought unsuitable
A barmaid and a farmer's son
But their love was indisputable.

They married in the spring
With bluebells in the wood
Cow parsley trimming all the lanes
They knew that life was good.

Home was a primitive cottage
Open fire and outside lav
The house was full of laughter
What more could anyone have?

She tried to be a farmer's wife
Though liked new clothes and make-up
When she returned from work at night
It was time for him to wake up.

And go and milk those beastly cows
Now paddling in the mud
'If I live here much longer
I'll start to chew the cud.'

His locks were long and beard to match
His jeans revealingly tight
Her neckline just a little too low
And hair unnaturally bright.

They started out as peacocks
Flamboyant plumage they carried
Difficult to become a peahen
And still be the girl he married.

A grand old aunt was visiting
She thought she must impress
She'd clean and tidy up the house
But the garden was a mess.

They partied all through summer
Bonfire, bottles, oil cans rusting
Debris completely covered the lawn

It really looked disgusting.

Evenings filled with music
Guitars and scented candles
Drifting, floating caftans
Ponytails and sandals.

She'd cook a lovely Sunday lunch
And lay a pretty table
They probably won't notice
That she can't muck out a stable.

They all had beautiful gardens
With fragrant flowers to cut
Winter isn't the best time
But they would still think her a slut.

Please help me God do something
Though not religious, she prayed
She imagined the rubbish magicked away
And turf all neatly laid.

She pulled the curtains back next day
To reveal a shimmering light
A soft covering of snow
Was glistening and white.

The grand aunt alighted from her car
'Oh, doesn't the garden look pretty,'
It even transformed the stable yard
Which was particularly shitty.

Oh thank you, whoever you are
For making everything fine
I knew you did kind little miracles
Like water into wine.

Jacqueline Longley

Not One, But Many Things

I am the champion, the protector,
the one you can trust to be there
When life brings along streams of worry,
I stand firm and shield you with care.
Then, when harm is pushed clean away
I'll stand guard by your side like before
And seeing your problems before they arise
they are easily kept from the door.

I am your champion, your guide in the world
and will listen whatever the hour,
For my place in life is to love and protect,
being endowed with the greatest of power.

I am the healer who washes out hurt
when you fall in your everyday play,
Then kiss away tears when you're frightened
and make all bad things go away.

I am the one who will hold tight your
hand in the dark so you won't walk alone,
And always I'm there when you need me,
I am with you, you're not on your own.

I am the healer who tries mending a heart
when another one tears at it so,
My power is strong, come, sit close by me,
you know that I won't let you go.

I'll feed into you all the love in my heart
then when the pain goes you will find,
In the warmth of the sunshine tomorrow,
you'll leave tears and sadness behind.

I'm the magician who conjures up spells
from an everyday sort of a book,
Holding dreams when you're quiet and thoughtful
and really, you don't need to look
Because magic I bring with the wave of a hand
which fills you with laughter, and then
As I watch how my happiness spell
spreads around bringing more laughter again.

I am the sparkle and wonder and awe,
a magical mix every day,
A magician, whatever the moment, and
knowing just what to say when the spell is complete
And I've captured your heart, and
I hold you a while in my hand,
For the magic appeared right in front of your eyes
just like your magician had planned.

I am your comfort, your teacher,
I have answers to puzzles galore,
All your molehills which turn into mountains
and there could be others I'm sure,
But just now, the little ones causing the stress
are not quite as large as you'll see
because I have answers to problems
I'll sort it, leave it to me.

I am a multitude, so many things,
all wrapped in a mother's disguise,
Taking you forward, showing you how,
like the owl with its large watchful eyes,
Seeing all things which surround you,
no matter whatever their size,
I'm all of your champions rolled into one
because, just like the owl, I am wise.

Rosie Oakes

Which Way To Go?

As I journey along life's highway,
The road well travelled and worn,
Many junctions and crossroads encountered,
Which one to take? I feel torn.

Which one will lead to disaster
And which to a life free from care?
Just give me a sign I can follow,
And one day I hope I'll get there.

Christine Nolan

On The Square

No matter who we are
And no matter what we do
We all have a special memory
Of a place
That we've passed through

The one place
I remember
With its statued lions so rare
Filled my mind with interest
As I rested
On the square

The pigeons by the fountain
Added charm to the morning air
And though the place was crowded
I sensed
A kind of magic
On that square

The people spoke of Wollaton Park
The arboretum
And the deer
They talked about the museum
And the best pubs
For a beer

Broadmarsh and the Victoria Centre
Were favourite shopping trips
And they came highly recommended
From every passing
Stranger's lips

I remembered the poets corner
Newstead Abbey
And the River Trent
And I recalled the university
Where all the scholars went

Then came to my mind
The castle
Steeped in history

Bad and good
With its origin
Of Maid Marion
And the famous
Robin Hood

Yes
The one place I remember
With its statued lions
So very rare
Filled my mind
With interest
As I rested
On the square.

Eddie Jepson

Yorkshire Relish

White Rose county - capital is York
A place of good and kindly folk
Rolling Wolds of vivid green -
Make for sure a pretty scene
But it's at the coast we like it most
Cliff top views and harbours grand
Fish and chips and golden sands
Lean roast beef and Yorkshire pud -
Does us all the world of good!
Whitby's bracing, Scarborough's bright -
And Fileys Brigg is a marvellous sight
Sewerby's gardens - looking fine
A splendid place to spend some time
Old Town Brid and the Yorkshire Belle
Treasured days we've known so well
And happy memories fond and dear
Of times we've rowed on Hornsea Mere
When it's time to go home, we may shed a tear
But there's always a chance -
We can come back next year.

G K Raynes

Wishing

I'd be the bravest soldier
In the army, oh the best,
Marching proudly on parade
With medals on me chest;
But when the cannons roared
And they're shooting everyone,
I think that I should take me kit
And up and bloody run!

The greatest surgeon I shall be
A man of world renown;
Saving lives and winning fame
And cheered from town to town;
But when I opened up someone
And saw what's in their core,
I think that I should either faint
Or vomit on the floor!

An airman bold I think I'll be,
In me aircraft, flying high;
Doing loops and barrel rolls
Across the wide blue sky;
But when the old Red Baron came
To initiate some fights,
'Tis then, I think, that I'd recall
That I'm afraid of heights!

A captain and a privateer
Is what I'd like to be;
Seizing foreign cargoes
From ships across the sea;
But when the warships closed in fast,
And cannons blasted shot;
Oh dear, perhaps a privateer
Is what I'd rather not!

A firefighter I should be,
Rushing through the streets,
With horns a-blaring loudly;
Saving lives and other feats;
'Twould be a great ambition,

A firefighter to aspire,
Except that I am quite afraid
Of anything like fire!

Soldier, surgeon, airman,
Fireman or privateer;
I haven't got the wherewithal
To make my new career;
Alas, those men I'll never be,
All heroes to this nation;
I'll just go back to me mundane job
In bomb deactivation!

John Bliven Morin

Holiday Cream

On your way, on your way
I will take you on a holiday

Florida crease, Miami beach
Manhattan, Birmingham, Leeds,
lunch in Munich, a dinner in Kiev
the bay of Bombay, and lots of leave
I will have lots and lots of leave for you

London Ben, Seattle den
Birmingham malls and Melbourne stalls
the Gaba ground, Caribbean sound
the Brazil ball and Vatican so so small

Southampton crease, Northampton dreeze
and Rio de Janeiro breeze
we will have Rio de Janeiro breeze
and then Serengeti spice and Machupichhu ancient life

the Arctic ice, Antarctic dice
the Barcelona blast, 777 very fast
then a dinner in Rome
and back to our sweet Indian home

back to our sweet, sweet home.

Amitabh Kumar

The Waders At Padstow Bay

They fly above the sandy dunes
That overlook the bay,
Where skylarks sing their pretty tunes,
The summer on its way.
But in the winter when the tide
Surges up on high,
Returning waders circle wide,
Then low down in the sky.

From whence might hail - these tiny wing,
Skipping o'er the squall,
The windswept waves the storms that bring,
Defying one and all.
In sand-wrest grasses - wap'n weave.
That cling the ocean door,
Their chosen nest the tide perceive,
Each spring upon the floor.

But when the ocean risen high
Plunges on the rocks,
Each mighty wave that meets the sky,
The waders come in flocks,
And plovers just a brace or two,
Depending on their kind,
The drying sand the tide renew,
Feeding as they find.

The strains that bend the ocean's swell,
Thundering on the bar,
The howling wind the trees train well,
Persuading just this far,
You hear the ocean's constant hiss,
The roar of a tireless sea,
Inside each roller never miss,
Ethereal and free.

That's how I see their tiny wings
When they flit among the spray,
Curving, grey-green, menacing,
Waders on their way.
They seem so safe amidst the brine,

Darting to and fro,
Like darting leaf so that they can dine,
The drying sands below.

And if you care to look inland,
More birdlife you can tell,
Behind the dunes beyond the sand,
Where other plovers dwell.
A different kind - of bigger wing,
A crest upon their head,
When farmers plough - keep following,
Ensure their young are fed . . .

Tom Ritchie

Trees

I look out of my window
All I can see
Is tree after tree
Waving at me
The beauty
The expanse
A plethora of green
They're huge
They're old
The history they hold
I expect they could tell a tale or two
If they could speak, and I only knew
The decades or centuries
As time has gone by
Still they are growing towards the sky
They wave in the wind
And smile in the sun
They feed in the rain
Displaying their leaves
Rich green and delightful
But still they grow
And the more they know.

Theresa Hartley-Mace

Travelling A Compilation

At Bell's Beach in Victoria we are pleased to stay
No cares, no worries, all faded away.
Watching the birds on this glorious day,
Viewing the excitement the waves can display.
Surfers out there braving the cold
For the chance to conquer the waves that unfold.
As we travel along the Great Ocean Road
Spectacular scenery begins to unfold,
London Bridge, the 12 Apostles, to name but a few
We look on in awe so much to see and to do.
Taking our time going from place to place
Seeing this great country we can never replace.
Diverse, so amazing, all wrapped in one
Our country for sure, cannot be outdone.
Beautiful sunrises to greet the day
Brings joy to my heart I am pleased to say,
So lucky to see these wondrous sights
They are truly magical, full of delight.

Dappled light filters through the trees
I feel the coolness of a gentle breeze,
Then walking down the track today
We came across a koala, sleeping away
High up in his gum tree as safe as could be.
To catch this rare sight was a real treat for me.
Wattle trees out in blossom throughout the bush
Mingled with river gums, oh so lush.
Blankets of pollen lay on the ground
Walking over it the smell was profound.
Honey went down to the river to drink
Gave me time to reflect, rest and think.
Here at Cobram enjoying the Murray
How could you ever be in a hurry?
As I sit there beneath the white gum tree
Overlooking the Murray, what a sight to see.
Knowing that in a few days
I will be back in Tassie and its wonderful ways.
This excitement of going back to where my heart belongs
I can feel the pull, oh so strong.

Now here I am at Myrtle park
Listening to the birds' merry lark
The babbling brook goes running by
Ah this scene of myrtle and pine, and the bright blue skies
Soft light filtering on the ferns by the stream
So picturesque, if you know what I mean.
I watch the grass doing its lively dance
Kissed by the breeze, when given the chance.
Platypus raise their shy little heads
Splash, then retreat to their own river beds.

Karen Holm

Beaches

The sun is shining, the birds are singing
The wind is blowing, the leaves swinging
If only all days were like this
Days you don't want to miss

The waves vanishing on the sand
Walking together, holding hands
Picnics on the beach, walking round the bay
Happy to be together in each other's arms
Not having to speak, nothing to say
But enjoying the beach, the day and nature's charms

The children laugh, scream and squeal
If only time could stand still
Ice cream, donkeys, Punch and Jude
Candyfloss, amusements, postcards galore - oh how rude!
Paddling in the sea, sandcastles in the sand
The mobile doughnut stands
Fish and chips on the wall
Listening to the seagulls call
Blankets on the beach
Lying together - just within reach

Time to tidy up, go home, the end of the fun
Starting again with tomorrow's sun.

Sandy Baudrey

Learning

Every day a child is born
With expectations brought upon
Wondering what the future holds
For the young becoming old

Whispering voices can be heard
As infants learn to speak first words
Curious eyes see all around
The different things that surround

Reaching out and taking steps
Learning to explore comes next
With parents they sit and look
At colour, word and number books

Sentences will come about
And when they do, just look out
Children learn to take command
For the things that they demand

Parents laying down the rules
The children, being their pupils
Separating right from wrong
Help the weak become strong

Children start their first school term
There are many things for them to learn
Reading and writing are just a few
There's the alphabet and spelling too

Teaching them to be creative
Helping them become more positive
There are so many things for them to learn
Throughout the years of their school terms

We go to school for education
To gain knowledge and qualification
Learning is a daily chore
Preparing us for the future

Reaching the age of responsibility
Using our knowledge and showing our ability
Get a job and earn some pay

Into the future, we make our way

Taking control of situations
Dealing with any complications
There are so many things for us to learn
To make our futures strong and stern

Having children of our own
Their futures are not yet known
Let them know that we are there
To give support, love and care.

Barbara C Perkins

Baby It's You

I sold my little sister,
To the guy who lives next door.
I sold my little brother,
To someone at the store.
I sold my dog, I sold my cat, I sold my baby snake,
My parents found the house cleaned out,
And screamed, 'For goodness sake.'
They didn't like my business deals,
It made their tempers rise,
They screamed, and yelled and carried on,
But it's just free enterprise.
I had to buy my brother back,
And my sister too.
It cost me more than they were worth,
But what was I to do?
I'll never try that stunt again,
I know I went too far,
So I'm working on a brand new deal,
To sell someone our car.
He offered me one dollar,
But I worked him up to three,
I can't wait to see my mommy's face,
Won't she be proud of me?

Jay Berkowitz

Moth-Eaten

Our silver-haired old dad changed since Mum went away.
Oh, she didn't go to Heaven,
she ran off with the insurance man in his Ford Capri!
Dad said, 'She'll soon be back, wait and see!'
That was in 1963.
He's become a recluse, a miser with any excuse to stay in
and not spend his money, which he keeps in a special belt,
he pats it affectionately every single day.
Now he's paranoid about *moths*
and spends hours planning their demise.
'They sneak up on you in the dark of night
and chomp away on my jumpers and ties,
they've eaten socks, hankies and even some tablecloths!'
Mothballs he buys in bulk, we just laugh and watch him sulk.
These moths must be special as he's put moth balls in the loo!
So these *alien* moths can eat porcelain too?

Suddenly he's changed! Gone the money belt, gone the thrift,
he's using 'Just for Men' on his silver locks.
To see him now a pseudo brunette rather shocks.
The change is swift. His old boots banished to the shed
as he wears trendy moccasins instead.
What's going on? We're all in a *tizz*.

The secret's out! He's met an exotic dancer
called Dolorez from Cadiz.
He discovered she was Doreen from Salford
and was spending his money in a whizz!
Dad wished her adios 'cos he wasn't as daft as he looked, now he's booked
a scenic tour of the Canadian Rockies.
He's bought new boots and removed her photo from his bedside table,
replacing her with a signed one of Betty Grable.
We bought him a new suitcase on wheels. He frowned,
'I'll take it to ASDA a couple of times to see how it feels.
'A digital camera? No thank you,
I've got one with film as it should be, on reels!'
Will there be exotic dancers in the Rockies
with names he can't spell?
Will he and Mum get together? Who can tell?
We bought him a new wallet all shiny with his money

counted in sequence.
He put her photo in it. 'I'll get her back one day,
I'll not be beaten.'
He had to throw away his old wallet because it was moth-eaten!
He doesn't know it but we sent Mum his itinerary just in case.
He still loves her and the insurance man didn't last long. Neither did the
Ford Capri.
Now we wave him off, new suitcase, wallet, boots
and now will have to simply wait and see.

Joyce Hefti-Whitney

Death And Resurrection

Your chocolate brown eyes pierce my soul
and in that minute I am made whole!
After liquid oromorph and morphine patches
my mind takes time to heal the scratches
of Dad's clawing, grasping, clasping hands.

No sleep only dozing and answering the phone
I hear your serious tone,
assertive and clear
so far yet so near!

In the surgery after his death
and the funeral
the house cleared
I cheered that I saw to it all.

I had to call
'Can I see you please?'
'Yes when?'
'How about this afternoon?'
'Yes that sounds fine.'

Then the dead line.

Brown eyes pierce my soul
my inner core you have made whole . . .
Brown eyes ask me some more soul-searching questions.

Elizabeth Scott

Helping Hands

What is the point in fighting?
What is the point in war?
What is the point of hurting?
What do we do it for?
Why are some people so cruel,
and hurt other people so much
when there are some people in this world
who have such a caring touch?
The world could be a much better place,
If everyone gave a helping hand,
If everyone agreed to help each other
it could be a much better land.
There are some people in this world
who have everything they ever need,
and others in this life
who just pray for a few crops when they plant a seed.
Animals are slowly disappearing,
in years to come some will be a distant memory.
Rainforests are failing every year
and will soon become empty,
if you are fortunate to have more than another
don't hesitate to share.
Some people aren't as lucky as others
but it doesn't mean they don't care.
Spare a thought from time to time
for those who have no home,
for those who have no family
and for those who are all alone.
A friendly smile is all someone might need,
a shoulder to cry on,
words of advice
or a secret they are carrying to be freed.
When there is love there is pain,
where there is sunshine there is rain,
where there is hurt there is light,
where there is hunger there is fight.
Help one another and others never forget.
Mock hurt and be cruel and you'll always regret.
For every tear there is a smile,

for every child that laughs it makes it all worthwhile.
So when you feel low and you think your life is bad,
just look at the world and try and be glad.
Try and teach your children right from wrong
and one day all the bad things in this world might all be gone!

Trudy Shepherd

Cat Lovers

They steal into our hearts
And dominate our lives.
They knead us with their paws
And melt us with their eyes.
They can claw our curtains
Or rip our rugs to bits,
Their habits are quite certain
To give us forty fits.
They're choosy what they eat,
But don't mind catching birds,
And quickly fall asleep
Despite our angry words.
Their fur is left around
For anyone to sit on,
They rub against our legs
To demonstrate affection.
They often cost us money
To keep them in good health,
But as long as we have them
Who cares so much for wealth?
All they want from us
Is tender, loving care,
And they are quite content
With our home to share.
But when they have to leave us
Feeling broken hearted,
We shall miss the friend
From whom we have been parted.

Barbara Fuller

Please, Mr Conductor

A lightning express from a station so grand
Had just started on its way
Most of the passengers who were on board
Seemed to be happy and gay
A little boy sat on a seat by himself
He was reading a letter he had
'Twas plain to be seen by the tears in his eyes
The contents of it made him sad

A stern old conductor then started to take
The tickets from everyone there
Till finally passing the seat of the boy
He gruffly demanded his fare
'I haven't a ticket,' the boy then replied
'But I'll pay you back some day.'
'I must put you off at the next station then,'
But stopped when he heard the boy say,

'Please, Mr Conductor, don't put me off the train
The best friend I have in the world, Sir,
Is waiting for me in pain
She's expected to die any moment
She may not live through the day
And I want to bid Mother goodbye, Sir,
Before God takes her away

As Mother was ailing before I left home
And needed a doctor's care
I went to the city, employment to find
But I couldn't get any work there
This morning a letter from sister arrived,
'Come home, Mother's dying,' it did say
And that is the reason I am anxious to ride
Though I haven't the money to pay.'

A little girl sitting nearby then exchanged,
'If you put that boy off, it's a shame,'
And taking his hat a collection was made
And soon paid his fare on the train

'I'm obliged to you, Miss, for your kindness,' said he

'You're welcome,' said she, 'never fear.'
Each time the conductor passed by that carriage
That boy's words would ring in his ears

'Please, Mr Conductor . . .'

Bonnie Austin

Woolworths

How sad that Woolworth is no more
We will miss this special store,
I remember when I was small
Whatever you needed, Woolworth sold it all.
Tools for all that carpentry,
Cups and saucers for that cup of tea,
Cheese cut for you by the slice,
Thick rashers of bacon that would fry up nice,
Brushes and combs and slides for your hair,
Curlers and shampoo every kind you'd find there,
Envelopes, writing pads to write that letter,
Aspirin and cough mixture to make you feel better,
Birthday cards to send to your family and friends,
Ribbons and lace and cottons to mend,
Buttons and pop studs and coloured pens,
Socks and plimsoles and children's clothes,
All neat and tidy hung up in rows,
Toys for babies, games for boys,
Little girls' dolls that made a *Mama* noise,
Gardening tools, weed killer, seeds too,
Aprons and gloves and paper for the loo,
The sweet counter was a child's delight,
Sweets of every kind to chew on a Saturday night,
A café where you could have jelly, cake and tea,
A wonderful treat for a child like me,
But Woolworths changed as the years went by,
The sixpenny store no more,
But although the prices increased through the years,
We shall miss this special store.

Christine Corby

My Bicycle

I bought this bike for half a crown
off Mr Baker 'cross the road,
A grey and sturdy upright bike
with no accessories . . .
no gears no pump no saddle bag,
and yet I was so proud
when cycling up and down the street,
Sat upright on my upright bike.
I was in Heaven
in the year nineteen forty-seven!

And then I cycled to the town
and parked my bike outside The Post,
stood upright in the gutter,
and went inside and bought a stamp
then raced back home at such a speed!
I was in Heaven
in the year nineteen forty-seven!

When I got home I parked the bike
against the entry wall
and looked at it . . . and looked again!
It had a pump and saddle bag
and gears and lots of other things!
Oh Lord, I'd taken someone's bike,
I'd stolen someone else's bike!
So back I raced down to the town
and saw my bike outside The Post
stood upright in the gutter
and quickly swapped the similar bikes,
then gingerly walked up the street
until I reached the corner,
where I looked back to see a man
and policeman hurrying to The Post.
What would the poor man say?
What would the policeman think . . . ?
of being dragged to view a bike,
a stolen bike . . . still standing there?

I thought I must keep out of this,

and with a smile raced back for home,
sat upright on my upright bike.
I was in Heaven
in the year nineteen forty-seven!

Leonard Jeffries

Repeat Performance

He wore white and moved
Just a little ahead
Through the long grasses,
Then between the trees
Just out of focus,
On vision's edge,
Just a little ahead.

He was white as a cricketer
And moved silently,
Always a little ahead
Just out of range.

Tiaras of pollen
Remained on the plantains
He passed, without stirring;
Crickets whirred, unmoved.
He hurried with some set purpose,
A recurring theme
Never to be caught up,
No drawing level,
No hand on the shoulder,
Just a little ahead,
Just a trick of the light.

When evening comes
He will be there again
With his long-forgotten reason
For hurrying
Just a little ahead.
It is his time of year.

E Hogg

An Encounter With A Monument

While travelling alone down a lonely way
I saw a man standing on the frontage
Of his house which was situated on a hilly bay;
And where he stood was a coign of vantage;
He was tall and gallant, his complexion was fair;
And that morning, he was looking happy and gay;
He waved at me and I waved back at him
Though the atmosphere was so misty and dim;
In excitement, I greeted him, 'Good morning Sir'
And expected something vice versa;
But there was no reply till the morning sun shone;
Then a bitch came in sight gnawing at a bone,
And then I thought, maybe he couldn't hear me
From that range, or that he wasn't listening attentively;
I decided to advance to where he stood;
I noticed that he was still smiling for good
And that his hands that were in the air,
As if they were raised up at once in pair;
As if he was waving them never did sway;
I was sure they would stay still like that all day;
No wonder he neither moved his body nor his head
To all the soothing words I had said;
Then I paused and mused a moment
Behold, the man was a monument!
Could it be the work of the medieval Michelangelo
That such a monument should deceive me so?

On the torso of the monument was an epitaph
Which read *You passing there, this is my cenotaph;*
In life, I was charitable, well mannered and kind;
But now I'm immobile, ever smiling and blind
I realised, the man I thought handsome and brave
Was just a decaying dust lying in his grave;
Then it dawned on me; such time I had spent
In trying to meddle with a mere monument;
Yet I prefer smiling at a smiling statue, non-living
To encountering a stony face of a living being.

Raymond Uyok

Shakespearean Dream

It is a dark and stormy night -
The tempest roars with all its might;
A winter's tale indeed - just as
you like it. Filled with verse that has
so much ado about nothing - much;
Love's labour's lost, so please don't touch
the merry wives of Windsor. Say
two gentlemen came by today
from somewhere - p'rhaps Verona, yes?
They asked for Troilus, then for Cress,
then further asked me if I knew
about the taming of the shrew!
P'rhaps the full moon's made me ill
or e'en Twelfth Night - or what you will?
Pray, help! This dream on Midsummer's Night
won't stop. Don't laugh! Don't mock my fright!
I dream of a merchant from Venice hence
and, measure for measure, I can't make sense
of the comedy of errors. And then, to boot,
King John has arrived with a friend and a flute
of champagne, which we share. Cymbeline (how absurd)
got really quite drunk -and shot Richard the Third.
Now Henry the Sixth has shown up in three parts
and Romeo and Juliet tug at our hearts,
and Titus Andronicus - (Cor! What a beast!) -
has invited King Lear and Othello to feast
on some ham(let) - but let us not dither and dally -
Coriolanus and Caesar await down the alley!
Pericles taunts poor King Henry the Fourth -
(who's now of two minds - and two parts) - and up north
King Richard the Second is reading Macbeth
while King Henry the Eighth puts his wives all to death,
and Timon of Athens meets Cleo and Tony
while Henry the Fifth has a fall from his pony -
What a dream! What a mess! But do not despair;
All's well that ends well, I assure you, so there!

Yes, a dream of all dreams - I'm still in a daze -
but at least now I know all the names of the plays!

Amanda Hyatt

A Whistling Kettle

Albeit I cannot knock it
A percolator in its socket
Makes good gunge for those who stock it
But it isn't tea.
Morning coffee, smooth or lumpy
Tends to make the drinker grumpy
Decaffeinated makes them jumpy
As is plain to see.
A whistling kettle in fine fettle
Wakes you up to grasp the nettle
Who then, but no one, wouldn't settle
For some Rosie Lee?
Tea drinkers sipping sweet Darjeeling
Face the morrow-morn with feeling
With Tetley tea bags, PG Tips,
Various herbal nondescripts
Indian, Chinese, Earl Grey too
Including Brooke Bond's famous brew
Plus Tesco's reasonable attempt
To stifle awful dreams you've dreamt
You face the big world every day
Feeling like the first of May.
When tea plantations are abundant
Should whistling kettles be redundant
Just because some procreator
Buys a plug-in percolator?
If my old mum was Mother Hubbard
She'd know who stuffed me in this cupboard
Wrap the perc around his neck
Then when flat out upon the deck
Would clean me up, restore by Jove
My rightful place upon the stove.
Whistling once again with glee
I'd make a lovely cup of tea
Fragrant as a rose's petal
Made only by a whistling kettle.

Phil Saunders

30

The Rescue Dog

When my old dog died
He was fourteen years old
From sheepdog to RSPCA
His life had been full

He didn't like other dogs
Only people, you see;
A hard life and a long one,
Ending with me

As I walk my new dog
He seems without care,
But don't forget where he came from
And why he was there

For some time I've looked
For familiar signs -
How Thomas behaved
While he was mine

At long last I realise
Taffy's unique
He loves dogs and people -
If only he could speak

But his looks say it all
'I'm here and I'm me;
Forget Thomas, I love you -
Oh why can't you see?'

Beautiful, gentle,
Obedient, clean,
Affectionate, cheerful -
Is that what you mean?

His innocent collie face
Seems to say,
'Please forget him and love me,
I need to stay . . .'

Diana Price

31

Down Our Way

Down those streets we often strolled
Streets which were not paved with gold
Tomorrow waited at the end of each day
There was lots of fun, down our way.

Terraced houses, roofs of slate
Bottles of orange from the milkman's crate
Everything was good, life was okay
There was lots of fun, down our way.

The swimming pool, the boating lake
The sun was beaming at daybreak
There as exuberance, we could not delay
There was lots of fun, down our way.

Wintertime failed to stop our fun
Snowmen quickly melted under the sun
Sometimes those clouds could be grey
There was lots of fun, down our way.

On the ochre pitch we could be found
A bunch of lads kicking a ball around
I have to say there was talent on display
There was lots of fun, down our way.

We were youngsters making great strides
Upon the swings and down the slides
After the excitement, on the grass we'd lay
There was lots of fun, down our way.

We traipsed all over the local park
We carved our initials upon tree bark
There were lots of hours in which to play
There was lots of fun, down our way.

Down our way was really fine
Especially when basking in sunshine
Memories of which will always stay
There was lots of fun, down our way.

B W Ballard

Stopping By A Grassy Bank At Midday

I cycle down a country lane at noon,
Where kerbside flowers, banked by summertime,
Are shrouded by the oak, and ash, and lime,
This sunny, midday memory of June,

The green and yellow fullness of the fields;
A joy-filled blanket, full of light and sun,
Where leaves and petals, grass stems, bindweed run.
There grass banks wait for me to kick my heels.

A warm and sticky sunheat gently glows,
And rambling hills give way, where shadows lie,
To tree-filled vales. And blueness of the sky
Frames memories of where Frome River flows.

Church spires rise above the blackthorn hedge;
And elderflower scents the hedgerow gate
And notice of this summer's local fete,
And by my feet squat primroses and sedge.

A tractor's chuffing busily away;
The combines marching steadily along,
Behind the hedges, plaited with bird's song,
Are making plastic coated bales of hay.

My bike's enjoying resting in the sun,
Its faded paintwork - scratched - is how I feel.
(A spoke is loose and rattles on the wheel.)
A friend with whom I've oft enjoyed a run.

I look through shade and light along the way,
It rises up to meet the trees afar.
These chippings, basking in the melted tar,
They gently sleep in peace this sunny day.

The sun waits, just in case a cloud should pass,
The ragged robin - nodding gently there,
The road dirt - glinting with a rainbow's stare,
They clap as I get stiffly off the grass.

M C Thomas

You Can't Beat The Good Life

I am a saintly puss,
That's what I am,
I'm renowned for eating
Whatever I can.
My mission on Earth
Though is not just
To find food,
But to set an example
To all domestic cats
As a rule.
So here I am,
Sitting in the pink,
By a roasting fire
With only happy
Thoughts to think,
So why not be like me,
Not out in the freezing cold?
Living the good life
And still only eleven years old.

My master's eye is on me now,
Is that a dish
Of delicious food I espy?
Of course, it's chicken,
Only the best,
And after I've supped
I'll have a good rest.
Must keep my strength up,
For such is life,
Although there's no work,
I swear I feel tired.
So all you guys and gals,
Please take heed,
Just give your cat
The indoor life it needs.

D A Reddish

My Love

The yellow rape fields amongst the green,
A vast open landscape, not a soul to be seen . . .
But I feel him.

I feel the warm sun and breeze caressing my back . . .
Is that you, my love?

I walk along the beaten track,
A red admiral is in my path . . .
Its vivid target markings on its back . . .
Is that a sign from you, my love?

Crows caw in the trees, scare, panic and fly into the sky above . . .
Do they feel your presence too . . . my love?

I walk carefree and alone,
But I know you are with me, in this quiet and peace,
Left all my cares and worries at home,
A free spirit with you in nature, at this moment
Even though we are together, to a passerby . . . I look alone.

'You see we are not humans living a spiritual life,'
In the breeze, you whisper to me . . . my love . . .
'But spirits in a human guise
Me a husband . . . you my wife . . .'

And though, now my husband, you have left this mortal plane,
We are still connected by love, that will not wane . . . my dear.

Of death now, I have no fear,
For many lifetimes, our paths have crossed, loved and lost . . .

But we shall be together again, my love . . .
That is very clear . . .
There is no longer a reason to shed a tear . . .
For my love . . .
Until that time . . .
Everywhere . . .
I feel you near.

Deborah Harvey

35

Ocean Of Blue

In a place meant for two
We would look out to you
Oh great ocean of blue

With white horses astride
That obey the tide
Across your ocean of blue

I would admire every hour
Just like a flower
Sunrays that dangle with you

In a place meant for two
And hearts beat so true
We would gaze on your ocean of blue

And down by your shore
You beach we'd explore
Or your ocean of blue

And nature would say
Just walk out today
And gaze on your ocean of blue

We would watch the moon too
As it journeyed with you
You beautiful ocean of blue

As your waves arrive on shore
We would just wish for more
From you, oh ocean of blue

In a spot just for two
We would keep thinking of you
Oh you beautiful ocean of blue

We would be happy out there
Just for to share
Such a beautiful ocean of blue

George McAdam

Worrywart

Fear manifests into loneliness,
It's no disorder sitting here alone,
Sitting, waiting, praying for steadiness,
It won't happen today, I'm fearful to the bone.

Twenty-three files under my name,
Or are they above in an orderly fashion?
Definitely above, before the memories came,
Definitely below, when I lost all passion.

These colours that circle my constant view,
They've turned, spiralled into shades of grey.
You do understand that in my world nothing is true,
Often blue, sometimes ecru but never okay.

I've been to that school, that school of depression,
Blackness, flatness and a textbook so faithless,
Dark clouds and an overwhelming oppression,
You're taught and force fed what it is like to be utterly reckless.

You do understand that in my world everything is false,
My smile, my optimism, my love of the isle,
A mask from the darkest, sharpest mind without pulse,
I'm dead inside, mentally poisoned with biocide and,
Every step I take is dampening down my pride.

I look in the mirror to a reflection so hazy,
Dull eyes. Blank spirit. A lost bundle of imaginary lies,
A personal perception of someone beyond crazy,
Caught up and binded to a thought that cripplingly crucifies.

What is this thought? What is this thought?
You do understand that thoughts are hard to get out,
But this thought that twists my sanity about,
Is this thought that one day I'll be free,
Just one day I'll be ridded of the nickname
Worrywart!

Sarah Dawes

A Morning Scenario

The overcast sky was totally grey
As I set out on an eventful day

A gale was blowing, my fingers were numb
As I stood waiting for the bus to come

At last it arrived, some people got on
For our journey that had just begun

Until we had stopped to pick up some fares
Most drivers will stop, least the ones that care

Three people I saw, patiently waiting
The first a lady, with loud voice shouting.

In her hand she held out a ten pound note,
'I'll spend my winnings today on a coat.'

She said aloud, but things were not right
For a gust of wind blew with all its might

It snatched the note from her hand held tight
And carried it up, away out of sight.

She screamed out loud, 'Oh! What can I do?
My money has gone, who will help me, who?'

The driver waiting patiently then said,
'I don't know darling, just use your head,

Get on without it, or go, try and find,
It's all up to you, make up your mind.'

It's probably gone, as far as Rugby.
He revved up the engine, she could plainly see

He would wait no more, she quickly got on
Bought a ticket, the money had gone,

She realised now, easy come, easy go,
She told the others about the big blow.

Terry Daley

Barn Owl

A seam of trees, bright with the green of spring,
Joins the field and down.
Along its length, abroad on quiet wing,
The moon-pale barn owl flies.
In concentrated search he seeks to kill;
A symphony of flight,
Of arching, graceful, aerobatic skill,
Enchanting birders' eyes.

Swooping in the grass he seems to fail.
Swiftly rising up
His almost lazy turn resumes the trail.
A courser in his pride,
He banks across the trees to search the hill
Where grass is cropped and short.
And tumbles down. And strikes with deadly will,
A hunter satisfied.

Mantling his prey with wings spread wide
He gorges on his food.
Mayhap a hapless mouse which failed to hide
And so met its demise?
Aloft again, he backtracks down the vale
And disappears from sight.
The shoulder of the hill now hides this pale
Minerva's bird, this myth of owl-wise.

His territorial boundary was it led
Him? Brought him circling back?
A silent stir of air above a head,
The golden markings clear
On feathers' cruel beauty close at hand,
Those predatory claws.
Though fine delight we take in nature's land,
Nature is hard, and need, a ready bier.

Margaret Montgomery

England

I am sitting here, wondering why
the birds are flying in the sky.
Their wings they flap without a break -
I ask myself, *do they not ache?*
The bees are hungry, eyes are glued;
hunger strikes, they must have food.
They show their presence by giving a buzz,
oh little bee, please don't hurt us.

The pavement's cracked, the lawns need mowing,
the wheelie bins are overflowing.
Car alarm sounds, the noise is blaring,
neighbours don't look - it's not worth caring.
Gangs of kids stood drinking cider,
every one a potential joy rider.
Can you approach them? Can you hell!
They'll take you down and crack your shell.

This is England, we're used to this,
benefit fraudsters in the post office.
They're stood in line waiting for their giro,
the post office alarm their biro.
The good drop off, the bad survive -
the truthful lose, the liars thrive.
There's not much more that we can do -
the government, we need you!

I'm not alone, the majority feels
we've been let down by the wrong ideals.
So please, Prime Minister, don't you slack
and give the English their country back.
I know it's hard and takes a lot
but we're all proud of what we've got.
So it's about time we made a fuss
and give our country back to us.

Daniel Woodgate

Slow Down

The pace of life is so fast today,
Everything has to be there by yesterday.
Nationwide couriers around the clock,
Deadlines to meet by vans and lorries
On multi-drop.
Express trains and jet planes,
Delivering freight time schedules,
Fast turnaround, can't wait.

Catamarans and hovercraft
Skimming the waves,
You can be the other side of the
World in a couple of days.
Road and rail, sea and air,
Mayhem and congestion everywhere.

Cast you mind back on times gone past
When the pace of life wasn't so fast.
Horse-drawn boats and exercise,
No pollution filling the skies.
Milk cart and coalman, rag and bone,
Everything was delivered to your home.
Nosebag on, wait patiently, any leftovers
Could be used on the rose tree.

Slices of ham, a chat, and potted meat
From your friendly corner shop down
The street.
The butcher with legs of lamb,
The baker with cobs and blooms,
Toasted on a long wire fork on an open
Fire, unforgettable aroma fills the room.
All you have to do is take a day at a time,
The rest of your life will work out just fine.

Philip G Clark

In My Dreams

I lace up my boots, they need to be tight
To protect my ankles when I take flight
I pat down my dress, now I'm ready to go
I have nervous excitement but I don't let it show
Today I'll skate in the open air
With the sun on my face and the wind in my hair
The spectators are seated, they're waiting for me
I'll do all that I can to be the best I can be
I step onto the ice so smooth and white
My blades leave their mark, they cut like a knife
I skate to the spot, wait for the music to start
Once chance, one dream, one skate from the heart
The music begins and my heart starts to pound
I skate forwards and backwards, round and around
I pick up my speed as I'm ready to jump
My toe-pick goes down, I'm propelled up and up
I soar high in the air and twirl round and around
Then back down to the ice I land safe and sound
I do several more jumps, do the splits in the air
See the joy on the faces of the people there
I do everything I've been trained to do
Every landing is clean, every edge is true
I skate on and on, now the end is in sight
Just one element left which I hope will delight
Now I'm spinning around, how fast will I go?
I start off tall then I finish off low
My performance is over, I can do nothing more
I take my bow, leave the ice and wait for my score
But my skates have hung up for many a year
I never did jump, too great was my fear
But in my dreams when I skate I soar high in the air
With the sun on my face and the wind in my hair.

Carolyn Jones

A Book In A Day

They started with the paper,
Recycled? Yes indeed!
They cut it into pages
Linked together with a bead.
They looped cord around the cover,
(Painted red and black and gold),
Stuck on sequins, wool and ribbon
Added jewels that looked quite old!
Now they had to fill the pages
With words and works of art
A try at writing poetry
Was the hardest part.
Teacher said that they were learning
A very ancient craft;
Bookmaking and calligraphy
Poetry and art.
The wonder of book creating
No matter what their skill or age
Always brings a look of joy to all
As they carefully turn the page.
Modern technology has robbed them
Of the need for pen and ink
But to make a book, however plain,
Gives them a chance to think.
They think about the days gone by
When children were so poor;
They think of walking miles to school,
They think of wanting more.
And so to make a book in a day,
A trivial task to some,
Becomes a journey through an age,
A journey of learning through fun.

Judy Rochester

Mountain Man

(Who followed his dreams)

Mountain man, you left the crowd,
Turned your face to the long, shining cloud,
To vastness and freedom and rugged grandeur,
Leaving a world that was ever obscure;
Where songs of the forest's fast-flowing streams
Flow on in the glades and hollows of dreams.

The call of the mountains haunted your days,
A dream ever taking your eyes away;
Now you follow wild mountain trails
Where snowy peaks beckon above the dark vales;
Where thought is a leaf flung to the breeze
And the sigh If the wind an echo to seize
When silence and solitude make you their own
And the call of the mountains is for you alone.

I think of you there on the edge of night
Clinging to the shadow of the eagle's flight;
I think of you when the moon is high
And the stars so big they fill the sky,
With the wind in your hair and your dreams unfurled;
You never looked back to this other world.

Now they say you're a 'legend' - 'Still up there you know,
That mountain man from long ago.'
There are those who say you can still be seen
Where the songs of the forest's fast-flowing streams
Flow on in the glades and hollows of dreams;
Where the long, shining cloud is the face of your guide
And a heart doesn't need a safe place to hide
For the spirit of Freedom is there in your eyes,
Where you found your mountain paradise.

Colleen Biggins

Feel! It's Lady Springtime Showcase Playing On And On

(Dedicated to my perfectly emotionally, spiritually and physically presented sensuous Goddess and the sultrily beguiling yet unspeakably genuine appeal of the glorious Cannock Chase.)

This adorable springtime showcase in the affable air
seeing off the melting slush of insurmountable despair
our fair land's mild atmospheric feeling returns so alive
boisterous bees buzz unflustered in the hive

Who feels it's Lady Springtime Showcase playing
in the tree-tunnels of the alluring Chase? Who feels?
Whoever does not feel her is of a dying breed, dead
on their feet, navigating but a purposeless fleet

Discreetly the seemingly meek but boundless in
rare strength Lady Springtime Showcase fills in
the blanks as ant-soldiers' gusto pervades through
the Chase's ranks

Day in and day out while this springtime endeavour
crawls seductively on Mum Nature's skin and goes
hell-for-leather, knowing full well how it pleases the scribe
who yens for the squall of springtime's woodland tribe.

So, let it be known that her touch is so pure and tender
yet this lady transcending all mastery knows no surrender,
She is a springtime warrior in the beyondness of things' scope
enticing the Chase's tribal creatures to damn well elope

Elope with no qualms about tribal conventions or the
prospect of endless severe castigations, the footpaths are
there for priceless freedom to spree, let it all salivate slowly
upon crackling bended knee.

Steven Ilchev

Mind And Body And Spirit

I wonder why it's Man's desire, in constant need to go much higher
There never seems a time when he can settle down and be happy
The more we have the more we yearn, the less we want, the
more we learn
Appreciate what you have got, it doesn't have to be a lot.

I understand our time is short and days go flashing by
I understand that we're not meant to know the reasons why
How everything is opposite and juxtaposed itself
The paradox that life presents to make men yearn for wealth.

If truth be told my body wants the things like others do
My soul, however, only dreams of being next to you
My one true love, if you exist, I think not as I write
But if you do and our paths cross, I'll recognise your light.

The light I saw and bright it shone, has made me pause for thought
The words I wrote in prior verse were heaven sent, not bought
From deep inside, within my soul, subconsciously they flowed
And in them lay a message that might make your mind implode!

The message is that I'm not one, I'm two inside my head
A spirit that is roaming free, and mind that must be fed.
With this in mind I am prepared to shock you with more thought
But please believe I do not need your love or charm that's bought.

My spirit needs companionship, a soul who is the same
My mind, too, yearns for company for words outside my brain
These two prerequisites I have for happy to achieve
Not one person that I have met can give this, I believe.

An easy life breeds arrogance with no firm base to see
Your spirit may be good or bad, your mind might not be free
To understand the words I write, look deep inside your self,
It's just the want of company that makes men yearn for wealth.

Nicholas Hall

Towns

Are the children succeeding
In reading, in *Reading?*
Can you take a shower
Or eat a bun for fun
In *Bath?*
What can you do
In *Crewe*
When waiting in vain
For a train
In the rain?
Do folk in *Leeds*
Lead the way
And do the ravens
Still want to stay
By the Tower in *London?*
When in *Bristol*
Make sure your pistol
Is in Bristol fashion.
Do itches twitch
On the cricket pitch
Near *Ipswich?*
Do ladies take umbrage
Or just frown
When the men in *Cambridge*
Wear a gown
In the town?
Who can tell whether
Mother'd be better
When she is unwell
By going to dwell
In *Motherwell?*

Margaret Nixon

Ten Years Ago

I look around the house but no one's here
They've all left home those I love so dear
This house was once full of children's laughter
With bedtime stories and happy ever after
Those early mornings with all its rush
Filling children's school bags their quarrels such fuss
But there's so little time
I've washing and ironing meals to prepare
There will be those sleepless nights with their dreams that scare
I loved Christmas morning with all its noise
My happy children with all their toys
But now every room is so, so still
I remember that day I said I will
To my babies I gave life
A loving mother devoted wife
Looking back now as another year ends
There were so many twists turns and bends
My children all grown and gone
Me all alone to just simply carry on
Their daddy looked for pastures green
With another woman he had been seen
So in the years that lay ahead
I shall lie alone in my lonely bed
My life has been blessed in so many ways
And in my dreams I remember those days
Watching my young family grow steadfast
For as their mother's love forever will last
There were times when it was difficult I do confess
So my darling children each one of you I bless
For now the chapters will one by one unfold
Leaving me so many memories as I grow old.

Ann Hathaway

Introspection

Somewhere within me on an island place,
That's cold and lonely
As starlight on the sea,
My spirit kneels upon a breaking shore
Sifting the shingle for sad splinters
Of love and integrity.

I hold the splinters up to the light,
To the thundercloud light of the skies.
Then, afraid of the gathering storm of tears,
I turn from that lonely shore
And look out with guarded eyes,
Look out on the practical, day-lit world
And tell myself it will do,
Accept expediency,
Leave that obstinate spirit
On the lovely, lonely shore
To throw the shattered fragments of love,
Rejected, back to the sea.

Obstinate, inexpedient spirit,
Holding fast against
The claims of reason,
Landlocked in my mortality by unbelief,
Hoarding my fears and love against my will,
Oh Spirit, this is treason!
You gathered all those broken shards
And spread them out
To dry, deceptive, on the sands.
I stumble on them everywhere.
Oh be careful those whom I would love;
I have splinters in my hands.

Daffni Percival

At The End Of The Road

A house there is at the end of the road
where a man does live, he lives there alone.
The garden is wild, the windows are dull,
the curtains have fallen, they sit on the sill.
We'd watch him come; then he would go,
with his pack on his back, he'd walk down the road.
He'd be away for months and our life goes on,
we'd play in our garden, then lie in the sun.
His house is a mess, there's no paint on the frames,
it's an eyesore to us when we're playing our games.

The stranger returned, I knocked on his door,
he welcomed me in; we sat on the floor.
I then complained about the house he lived,
as I turned and looked he was unpacking his kit.
This man was no stranger, he was a soldier on leave,
'Don't pity my house, it's an anchor for me.'
With sand in his boots and mud on his back,
he rolled out his bed and ate from a pack.
'I come home to rest, my house is not bleak,
the floor is dry, it's a place I can sleep.

I choose this life, a soldier am I,
a guardian of freedom, for this I will die.
Don't cry for me or feel for my plight,
your future is safe; secure at night.
My life is my bond, loyalty I swear,
take comfort from this, a promise I declare,
I fight for my country; my God is my friend,
I don't ask for more, peace I defend.
There are many of us live at the end of a street,
don't judge what you see, wait till we meet.'

Dianne Audrey Daniels

50

The Coming Of Apophis

Near Earth objects terrify
Cutting through our space, they fly
Our gravity could pull them forth
Ready to shatter fragile Earth.

A million, billion megatons
Worse than every nuclear bomb
The skies will burn at a thousand degrees
Causing the boiling of the seas.

Our astronomers, scanning the skies
Have noted with shock, and with surprise -
That these objects were less than thrifty,
More than eight hundred and fifty!

All life on Earth will be destroyed
If we collide with an asteroid,
It could spell the end of us
Each one reduced to a pile of dust.

Could it ever come to this?
Yes! They've named it *Apophis!*
It could hit this century -
The end of you, the end of me!

Technology's our only hope,
Do our devices have the scope
To thwart the dread trajectory -
And prolong life for you and me?

Let us hope, and let us pray
That we will never see the day.
It has happened here before,
That's why there are no dinosaurs!

Gregor Cook

Life

When God made up this planet,
He had a few things on his mind,
For what he needed on his land,
Was for Man to be really kind.

Not to waste resources given,
Nor to idle on the way,
Just work to keep his place going,
Twenty four hours a day.

Don't take what isn't needed,
Leave some things behind,
Remember others follow,
That's the way of mankind.

We labour in the corn fields,
To produce our daily bread,
We need to know what's growing,
Before we go to our beds.

We are all part of this planet,
No matter what our creed,
Whether black or white it doesn't matter,
We just need to succeed.

We should work with one another,
Never thinking of a war,
It isn't what He wanted,
Peace is what we're for.

Go about your daily business,
With pride and not with shame,
Because when your life is over
We end up just the same. *Dead!*

Audrey Howden

The Credit Crunch

The credit crunch is now biting
With tough times ahead for all
All because some of the bankers
Took their 'eye off the ball'

Too keen to make their targets
And get their wad of dosh
They lent out many billions
To keep their lifestyles posh

Arranging substantial mortgages
Bought people lovely homes
Now they may be left with nothing
Unable to pay off all their loans

The companies are all folding
As the banks call in their debts
They have monthly outgoings
And the payments can't be met

From the figures made by Dalton
To the trucks at JCB
Throughout every industry
Hard times are plain to see

As always the surest job is an undertaker
Though it may be hit in the same way
Because though people will keep on dying
They may have no money left to pay

So if your position is still safe and sound
And you're still making a few bob
Be thankful and content if you can
As 100 people want your job!

Christopher Leith

Nature's Way

Think before you swat that fly,
And the work it does on Earth and why
The maggot that it was before
Eating nasty things galore.

It helps to clean the countryside
Eating all those things that died,
Without it we may not survive
Even hospitals use them to keep us alive.

Birds that fall from sky to die
Eggs are laid on by the fly,
Without it germs would multiply,
So think before you swat that fly.

Flies are food supply for birds and bats,
Which in turn are food for cats,
And so the food chain continues
Providing food for other menus.

So if we had a world without them,
Break the chain and nothing we could do about them.
Germs could take over and we could die,
So think before you swat that fly.

Flies are put there for a purpose,
We know that there can be a surplus
So be careful not to kill too many,
Or we may end up not having any.

Arrogance tells us we're the best
We're in that food chain like the rest
So if you wish to reign on high,
Just think before you swat that fly.

James Robert Proudlove

On Retirement

I finally said, 'That's enough'
Sixty-four years of work just to get by
It is time now to do what I want to do
To choose how to let my time fly.

Turn off the alarm, breakfast back in bed
Boot up my computer at leisure
Dress now for comfort, not smart office clothes
Enjoy my time, each moment to treasure.

As I snuggle back down I can hear
Mothers taking their children to school
And to workmen busy in sun's early glare
Whilst I can lay back and stay cool.

If I want to go out, I choose when
Do my chores whenever I want to
I can potter around my garden
Or just take a drive for the view

I can fit in appointments any time of day
I can go out on a mystery tour
I can just put my feet up and be lazy
But I'll never be bored that's for sure.

I have made out a list, many things to get done
Some important while others can wait
This will help me not to forget one,
At the end are the jobs that I hate.

I cross off what I've finished but others I'll add
Urgent phone calls or running repairs
Whatever I do now that I'm retired
I can do at my pace and be glad.

Sheila Bates

Big City

My city, concrete and stone
busy streets, all alone
the bustle of people
big church steeple
cars, buses and a bike
many folk, that look alike
shop windows that invite you in
charity workers shaking their tin
noise, fumes and pollution
the government trying to find a solution
pigeons prance without a care
men and women just stand and stare
market stalls with fresh produce
persuasive banter that tries to induce
offices, shops and high street banks
ladies doing surveys that receive no thanks
a busker strums on his old guitar
the music can be heard from afar
this is a day in the life of my city
it can be hectic, yet can be pretty
fast food joints and coffee shops
time for a latte with creamy tops
homeless folk sat by a door
big issue sellers for the poor
police sirens scream and wail
I'm off to the pub for some ale
CCTV that watches every move
break dancers busting a groove
time to go and head for home
cold and tired and all alone.

Karl Delaney

Andrew's A & E

As we sit
And wait
And wait
The room fills up
Through the night
As we sit
And wait
And wait
People
Come and go

With crews
In green
And nurses fair
Doctors running
Here and there
We wait
In queue
To be seen
And wait
And wait
And wait

And as we wait
Throughout the night
In silent anguish, pain
We wait
To be
Assessed . . .
And wait and wait
Again.

S A Brown

Saving Energy

Here are some things you may like to try
To save electricity so your bills aren't high
And to save our environment like the polar caps
To stop them melting and other mishaps
Or in years to come the sea will rise
It'll cover our land and be double the size
Everything on land would suffer
The floods will come in, the sea will get rougher
So listen and tell your parents or carers at home
And even your relatives or friends over the phone
To save electricity around their home . . .

Here are some things you may like to try
Turn out the lights when the sun's in the sky
Have a shower instead of a bath
It's much quicker and you'll have a laugh!
When Mum boils the kettle make sure it's not full
Wasted water is just left there to cool!
Switch off the plugs you don't use during the night
Ask if you're using energy-saving bulbs for your lights
Check your washing machine is washing at 30 degrees
Too much detergent will just make you sneeze!
Turn down your heating and insulate your loft and walls
Recycle your rubbish so production lines fall
Wait till the spring and hang out ya washing nice and high
Avoid using your tumble dryer to let your clothes dry

Just these few simple things could save our planet
And make our world right
Keep the polar caps floating together nice and tight!

Anne-Marie Howard

A Distant Roar

The shells and pebbles crunch
Beneath my feet as I walk alone across the empty beach.
In the distance roars a swollen, stormy sea
I am glad it is safely out of reach.
The winter wind moans at the craggy rocks
As I bend to peel off my yellow woollen socks,
The sea flicks and flotsam tosses through the air,
Its saltiness I taste upon my lips, it whips
My face and bounces my hair.

The sands are sparkling from
The retreating tide,
Hungry seagulls soar and scream raucously
And ringed plovers, turnstones, curlews race
Along the heaving shore
As gannets dip and dive pedantically.

Oh, this is a far cry from Milton Keynes,
Yes! Suddenly I am glad to be alive!
Free ephemerally from massive buildings,
Shops roaring in the crowds,
Concrete cows; tall walls
And distance myself; take 'time out' to shake
Those cobwebs from my head . . .
Clean away anger
This beach, my monastery for the day.
Another day,
I'll come and listen to the
Oceanic roar - some other day
When I'm not alone . . .

Judy Studd

Dear Mother Earth

Dear Mother Earth will you have a rebirth?
Trampled down by us humans in the past,
My generation could be the last.
Technology we thought was so great,
But all it caused was further greed and hate,
Polluting both the sea and clouds,
Mother Earth doesn't look so proud.
Your body has taken the punishment well,
But the effects of history starts to break down,
There's nothing here except concrete towns,
Mother Earth, soon all you have will go,
Soon you'll have nothing left to show.

Your destruction will be caused by ignorance and lies,
Turning the once tranquil air into darkened skies.
We choose not to see your signs and deafen your pleas,
As we continue to pollute and poison your blue seas.
Building, buildings so tall as to block out the sun,
Today's great architectures will be tomorrow's slum.

I have this dream where everything is green and we live in harmony,
For to live in peace and to co-exist with each other is surely the key.
For this generation will fight to put your wrongs to right,
For we will deal with your mistakes and try to clean up our lakes,
For we will deal with the lies and try to save our wonderful skies,
For we will deal with many things and the destruction it brings,
'Cause I don't want to see this wonderful and beautiful place,
Becomes nothing more than a spinning rock of waste in space.
For you should respect what you've got,
Before we end up destroying the entire lot.

N D Hawas

Desert

This desert is a wasteland
The lack of life is second
Only to the lack of sound
And as I stand and look around
I see nothing . . .
I hear nothing . . .
They're dead, these fields of silicone
All over-wrought and overgrown.
Any signs of real life are brief
I find myself caught up in grief
For so much space
Bereft of life
In such a place
With no respite
From miles and miles of ground up glass
I wonder how much further it can last
Rolling hill after rolling valley of broken microchips
That you can only cross in 'desert ships'.
The inhumidity and inhumanity is a pity
So I turn my back on this soulless, lifeless city
Its trains and trams, buses, cars
Its shops and nightclubs, restaurant bars
The information super-highway
Where everybody does it 'my way'
Phone and mobile, Sky and broadband
Tonne after megatonne of compounded sand
I've seen much of what the city offers
But I believe the world has more to proffer.

Jonathan Hobdell

Clichés

I never write in clichés,
I nip them in the bud.
I'll write from dawn to dusk
Without a break to chew the cud;
Although I'm no spring chicken
I'm as busy as a bee
Avoiding tiresome clichés,
They aren't my cup of tea.
Clichés rarely fit the bill,
A truth I take as read,
I'd ban the lot, call it a day
And put them all to bed!
Yet we still see them sprouting,
Spreading thick and fast,
Dead, linguistic dinosaurs,
Dull blasts from the past.
My feet are firmly on the ground,
I have no axe to grind,
And yet, if clichés win the day,
Then justice must be blind.
Every cliché's Greek to me,
They make my blood run cold,
And though they gild the lily,
All that glitters is not gold.
And so, when all is said and done,
I've got things off my chest
Without resort to clichés -
And that's the acid test!

Alan Millard

The Heartbeat Of A Country

(Bob Murphy MM, served with the Irish Gds 1940-46)

I know a man named Bob, who fought for you and me.
This man still stands tall, covered in history.
Joined the army as a young man back in 1940,
A well-set young man, played football and was rather sporty.

'So what makes the man special?' I hear the reader ask.
He wanted to help his country and so set bravely to his task.
Like thousands before him and after, he started rather shy,
Fully understanding at anytime there was a possibility he could die.

This legend won the military medal for valour in the field.
Inside this man's mind is a history waiting to be revealed.
Now time has taken its toll and Bob is not so steady,
But inside this man's heart I know he is ever ready.

I am so proud to know this man and his good lady, Doreen.
You do not have to be a soldier to understand what I mean.
These men and women still walk this land that is free,
Without them, our country would have a different history.

So I, for one, would like to thank them for giving up so much.
They are a part of history that I feel that I can touch.
As a soldier myself, I do fully understand
The expectations of a nation and the sacrifices they demand.

We still have brave men and women fighting for you and me,
Still in the name of Freedom and of Liberty.
So Bob has done his bit and kept us in the race,
Let us not let his history disappear without a trace.

Tom Roach

Compulsive Gamblers Beware

Gambling is a road to nowhere
It's full of dreams without a care

Compulsive gamblers often find themselves
In a web of destruction
It can be a fatal attraction

They fail to believe
It's themselves they deceive

When you bet blind
There's every chance you'll lose your mind

If you win it's not for long
Winnings are all soon gone

When they go to bet again
They find they lose it all the same

You cannot win it's a losing game
And it could send you completely insane

So don't be oblivious to those around
Don't bet and keep sound.

A compulsive gambler bets with money
he needs without a doubt,
To win money he can do without.

They know that it's a foolish game
But they do it time and time again
So do not find yourself in despair
Compulsive gamblers beware.

John Walker

Waking Thoughts

When the sun starts glinting in the eastern skies,
And the darkness of the night gradually disappears,
When we begin to wake to the opening of another day,
We should remember the opportunities we have wasted
down the years.

We should not allow these thoughts to fill us with sadness,
Nor let our hopes be buried in despair,
But look forward to the future with anticipation
As we fill our lungs with the fresh morning air.

Every successful life needs a vision,
And behind that vision there must be a plan,
If we are not prepared to make this work,
We shall continue to be an also ran.

Each day is a day of new opportunities,
A time when we can start our life anew,
This time there will be a need for resolution,
To do all the things we know that we should do.

So many of us have failed to do this in the past,
That is why so many of our lives lack satisfaction,
We might envy the success that others have enjoyed,
And this should make us realise that now is the time for action.

Otherwise, our waking thoughts will be filled with sadness,
And these thoughts should make us realise
Another day has come and brought new opportunities,
When the sun starts glinting in the eastern skies.

Ronald Martin

Happiness On A Mission

Feed your heart with thoughts sublime,
Then open-minded bliss is thine.
Feed your mind with clouds of doubt,
Then unhappiness reigns, despair just floats about.

B Wharmby

Pain Gates Posture And Poise

We arrived at nine-thirty on Wednesday morning,
All eagerly looking forward to learning
About the ups and downs of chronic pain,
Not a moment's peace for our tormented brain.
We were not let down or disappointed,
The knowledge we gleaned quickly mounted.
There were courses for pain and examples of pacing,
Open and closed pain gates, minds were racing.
Finding our limits and attainable goals,
Pacing, priorities and planning enfolds.
There was relaxing, posture, exercise and meditate,
All avenues were opened to help us relate
To personal needs leading to a weekly planner
That highlighted our cans and can'ts just like a scanner.
Communication was an absolute must,
Who can read minds? Just settle the dust.
Try not to confuse your thoughts with fact,
Get the story right and use your tact.
Trouble sleeping, what about Alison's read?
Booms, doors, escalators, numbers, where did it lead?
To a secret garden and as you opened the door,
We saw sunlit trees and a green-carpeted floor.
We were all encouraged to follow our dream,
Sat by that crystal clear, gurgling stream.
To our four tutors with such a sense of humour,
Thank you for lifting our load,
Maybe we're sorry school is over.

Barbara Jermyn

The Wait

I yearn to feel this wait removed
To fly away, each year, refused
They wait, so young, to run out free
Like rats in waves, the yacht they flee.

Christopher G Elliott

Celebrate The Dance

The nightingale who sings
Spreads her silken wings
Anticipates the flight
To soar with all her might
Will she celebrate the dance?

The robots now look small
So proud, the bird soars tall
Swooning and swaying
Dancing, then gliding
As she celebrates the dance!

The unicorns appear
Free will is always near
Parading a glorious flight
Round moon and stars so bright
Will you celebrate the dance?

Inhale the forceful wind
With each breath, and positive mind
As their spirits become one
Their souls join in the fun
Come celebrate the dance!

The fairy dust scatters
As the emerald one gathers
A fanfare in the sky
It sparkles from their eye
As they celebrate the dance!

Lorna Cameron

Chocolate

Chocolate is my only vice,
But chocolate tastes so very nice

But choc-o-late is full of fat,
My stomach used to be so flat

I'll give it up, reduce my waist,
But I'm addicted to the taste

So now, cold turkey I must face
A choc-free diet I'll embrace

There's nothing much for me to smile at,
I go on automatic pilot

Head for the fridge, I think I'll risk it
And take a little chocolate biscuit

It is no Picnic, makes me surly,
I crave a Mars or Curly-Wurly

But as I climb upon the scales
(You must try this, it never fails)

I see the weight that I have lost,
But it has come at such a cost

I do not know how long I can
Live as a chocolate-less man

But when I've curbed my waist inflation,
I think I'll have a Celebration!

Rob Barratt

I Can't Be Doing With That

I don't need a stately home
With gardens all around
I don't need an aeroplane
To take me off the ground.

I don't need a limousine
To take me to the shop
I don't need ten caterers
To cook my Sunday chop.

I don't need a bodyguard
To scare away my foes
I don't need a bunny girl
With hardly any clothes.

I don't need a swimming pool
To jump in when it's hot
I don't need a sailing crew
To take aboard my yacht.

I don't need to holiday
For six months of the year
I don't need a full-time slave
To carry all my gear.

I don't need a Harrods bag
For everyone to see
I don't need no caviar
So go and leave me be.

Shaun McEwan

Holidaying With Friends

Taking a walk along Epple Bay
Little hand holding mine
Daniel likes skipping and shows me the way
Open a bottle of wine

Ramsgate, Margate, holidaying is fun
A beach hut is the best
In England you don't always get the sun
But it's good to have a rest

The sand is wet so that must mean
The tide is going out
Clever little Bethany is keen
To show me all about

Lots of history to learn
Charles Dickens lived here
The beach is clean, the blue flag is out
Lifesaver, Paula, is always near

Nipping out for a drink and a laugh
We've had a busy day
Tony is a dad and a half
And will make sure the kids are OK

The sea air is good but I'm afraid
I must be on my way
Thank you, friends, I'd love to have stayed
What a happy holiday!

Josie Pepper

Shed No Tears

Shed no tears, my loved one, shed no tears for me,
Love is like the ocean, the enigmatic sea.
You can almost feel it, breathe it in the air,
Remember me always, and always, if you care.

I will come at break of day, I will come at noon,
You will remember me when they play our tune.
I will come in the evening, I will come at night,
You will remember me in mountains of great height.

As you walk in the garden amongst lovely flowers and trees,
You will remember me, that's what love decrees.
As you pass a waterfall tumbling with a mighty roar,
You will remember me and how I passed through Heaven's door.

As you stroll along a sandy shore taking in the sun,
Remember all the lovely things we've seen and done.
The moon, riding on the clouds, shedding on you her light,
Remember eagles, soaring in the wind, in graceful flight.

When the conversation sparkles with a particular turn of phrase,
Remember, my darling, those halcyon days.
You can almost touch me from the other side,
Not yet, my love, the time will come, we must abide.

Have no fear, we will meet, we will meet again,
Now you see me in your dreams, you ask, 'When?'
We do not know, the future is yet unseen,
You will remember me, love is not a might-have-been.

Irene Greenall

Monday Morning

At eight o'clock I hear a noise,
The men collect my bin,
Rattle and crash and thud,
Oh goodness! They make a din.

I look out of the window,
Bins left everywhere,
Bits of paper flying about,
They don't really care.

Mums come out looking harassed,
Children to get to school,
Sitting in the car impatiently,
The kids always late as a rule.

Neighbours hurrying to get to work,
Small children starting to cry,
Older people walking dogs,
Husbands waving goodbye.

Mums pushing pushchairs with three or four kids,
Vans delivering goods,
The postman whistling with a bag full of mail,
Teenagers pulling up their hoods.

Taxis driving by, waiting a while,
Taking their fare - who knows where,
Everyone busy, a hive of activity,
As I stand by the window and stare.

June Melbourn

Every Day Was Mother's Day

Each Saturday brought me my due pocket money
Before and then during the Second World War -
Days which were stringent in market economy;
When no child would think that it ought to be more.

I'd save up and visit a shop which sold china.
My eager legs took me as fast as could be.
The lady in charge of it could not be kinder
And brought out the treasures I wanted to see.

The things in that shop were not wartime 'utility' -
Plain, stark, unpainted, incredibly dull.
I'm puzzled today at the availability
So cheap at the price and a shop which was full.

A pot for the jam or a dish for the butter
Designed with bright fruit or a fine Jersey cow;
Something I thought would be loved by my mother
Was just the right present I'd carry home now.

When I look back, I can see she was sorry
I had not bought sweets or a book or a pen.
But when she'd 'reprove' me, I'd say not to worry
For I was quite happy to do without *them*.

So she had far more dishes and pots than she needed
All gently laid by in a cupboard;
But I hope that deep down in her heart I succeeded
To be the dear child she had mothered.

Edith Bright-Butler

Stop And Think

Sitting on the lamp post, watching the world below,
There was a young kestrel, wondering where to go.
Food was easy enough to find, if you knew where to look,
But to find and hold prime territory, now intelligence that took.

Sitting on the garden lawn, outside her mother's house,
A young lady looked up at the sky, and mournfully cried out.
O' where will I find a home, a place to call my own?
O' when will I find a friend, so I am no longer alone?

Sitting on the seabed, his tail wrapped tightly around a leaf,
The seahorse wishes to himself, that something could share his grief.
The grief of polluted water, of slowly losing your home,
And having no control over it, for a seahorse can't even moan.

Sitting on the office couch, slowly sipping organic tea,
The chief executive smiles, at the profits of his company.
No worries for me, he thinks, *for I have a beautiful home,*
A loving partner and clean water, I have no reason to groan.

Sitting on the leather sofa, in his own home territory,
He watches a young kestrel, and suddenly feels sorry.
Sorry for the young lady, who sits crying on the lawn,
Sorry for the seahorse, who may not see another dawn.

No longer sitting, he paces around the room,
Wondering to himself, how to bring joy to their gloom.
Then a thought strikes him, like none he's had before,
Why not share his profits, and bring some joy to all?

Stacey Mayer

The Beautiful Kate!

Black sapphires nestle in her hair
And in her eyebrows, too.
Her gentle smiles, so sweet to share,
Are blessings ever new.

So statuesque, with noble grace,
Each pose a memory . . .
She draws us near with just a gaze . . .
She's such a sight to see.

Her hair cascades like waterfalls
And glistens now and then . . .
And suddenly my heartbeat stalls,
Then starts I know not when.

Yet in those moments, time stood still,
When love was in the air . . .
When all at once I felt a thrill
That seemed beyond compare.

God blesses those who seek to please,
Who dress their best each day,
Who radiate a sense of peace
In all they do and say.

So I'll be thankful for each twirl,
So cheerful, chic and great . . .
Who is this truly lovely girl?
She's the beautiful Kate . . .

Denis Martindale

Mad

I think I'm going crazy,
I must be slightly mad.
I've started eating wallpaper,
It doesn't taste half bad.

I know I'm going barmy,
I am, I'm off my noodle.
I went to buy a guard dog
and bought a small French poodle.

I'm definitely wacko
and I've lost the plot,
I like to wear my flippers
when I'm in the bath a lot.

I'm nutty as a fruitcake,
I'm really off my head.
Last night a spaceship
full of Martians landed on my bed.

Yes, I'm cuckoo, crackers,
out of my tiny mind.
I should be in the Funny Farm
with more of my own kind.

Oh yes, I'm nuts and barking,
So completely bananas.
They locked me in a rubber room
in polka dot pyjamas.

Mark Andrew Bennett

The Charity Shop

Black shorts and an orange top,
Ellen goes looking for a charity shop.
Not in her 'neck of the woods' as usual,
It's down to Canterbury, she does her best as usual.

Ellen has a bundle of ladies fashion over her arm,
She hopes they will fit her obvious charms.

To find sizes to cover her middle-aged spread,
Oddments of skirts and tops, and a dress in red.

She espies a smart threesome, a three-piece suit,
In that ensemble, Ellen, you could look cute.
Into the changing rooms she flounces in,
She really does not know where to begin.

There are garments flying everywhere.
The assistant can only stand and stare.
'I'll get a bargain if it kills me.'
Five bargains later, Ellen doesn't give in, not she.

At two pounds an ensemble, a Christmas tree she does resemble
'I cannot resist, I love to have a good root.'
Her bank balance will suffer, but she buys the suit.
'Yes, in that little three-piece, I will look cute.'

Self-satisfied and duly placated,
That charity shop in Canterbury has left her elated.
She won't have a word said against this sort of shop.
'I like them very much and I'll shop until I drop.'

Ellen Spiring

Heavenly Hope

A cherub so small, insignificantly so
Would learn not to see, not to say, not to know
Not to be, not to want, or to whisper a groan
Just to sit, count the minutes,
In the dark all alone

But in the depths of the valley, this cherub was restored
Emotions and feelings no longer ignored
But the journey to freedom, was through darkness and fear
Anxiety and pain, remained always so near

But alas, there's a soul that with mine now does walk
Does share, does feel, does cry, does talk
Another lost cherub, that felt such great pain
Now together we stand, ne'er to suffer again.

Carole Spreddie

What Shape Is Peace?

What shape is peace? Can it be round?
And is it laid in hallowed ground?
Should peace have feathers like a dove?
Elusive, like the ways of love?

Is peace bright flowers that we've bought?
To compensate for scraps we've fought?
Or a fabric sticking plaster
To mask the scars of close disaster?

Is peace no gunfire in the night
Because the troops need sleep to fight?
Or streets bereft of bustling noise
For fear of meeting gangs of boys?

Will *Nessum Dorma* sung in style
Pacify the rank and file?
Or *Feed the World* dish out the rice
Without some costly sacrifice?

In truth peace comes from deep inside;
So as I've looked within, and cried,
And glimpsed; I had to drop
The finger pointing; blaming stop.

For in each place peace kits comes free;
Assembly's down to you and me;
So picture peace; each rare disguise
In tone of skin, creed, shape and size.

Martin Winbolt-Lewis

Curse

Within my heart beat a hundred love stories
Wishful thinking of a young girl's dream,
Inside my head a thousand images
Of happy ever afters that have never been.

My soul is but a broken mirror
A reflection once for all to see,
This distorted face on shards of glass
Sadly is no longer me.

Like a jigsaw of scattered pieces
I hold them all within my hand,
Yet with so many pieces missing
I will never understand,

Who I am, or where I'm going
Just a past to where I've been,
One I wish could be forgotten
That seems to haunt my every dream.

All I do is seem to question
This life I'm leading is false and fake,
Everything I want and yearn for
Is something sadly I cannot take.

The hurt inside plunges deeper
With every passing night and day,
Hoping God will come release me
From this curse, I can only pray.

Lisa Mills

Mad

I think I'm going crazy,
I must be slightly mad.
I've started eating wallpaper,
It doesn't taste half bad.

I know I'm going barmy,
I am, I'm off my noodle.
I went to buy a guard dog
and bought a small French poodle.

I'm definitely wacko
and I've lost the plot,
I like to wear my flippers
when I'm in the bath a lot.

I'm nutty as a fruitcake,
I'm really off my head.
Last night a spaceship
full of Martians landed on my bed.

Yes, I'm cuckoo, crackers,
out of my tiny mind.
I should be in the Funny Farm
with more of my own kind.

Oh yes, I'm nuts and barking,
So completely bananas.
They locked me in a rubber room
in polka dot pyjamas.

Mark Andrew Bennett

Grandad Ford

My grandad Ford is never a bore
He makes me laugh, and laugh even more.
He'd like to live till he's a hundred and eight
And I'm sure he will get there, it's simply his fate.
He'll most likely stay longer, we'll wait and see
Who knows, he might even outlive me.
His stories of the war are of great interest
And he's never, well maybe, sometimes quite a pest.
I imagine Grandad was a charmer with the ladies
But I don't think at all he has told them about his rabies
(only joking!)
My grandad Ford has made us all very proud
Especially a special grandma who is up in the clouds
He brightens everyone with his funny and hard-working personality every
day,
And because of this I would like to say
He gives all his family so much happiness
Throughout all of our lives
I hope he continues to have a joyful life
Even through all of his pain and strife.
We all appreciate everything he does too
And I would like him to know that, 'we love you.'
Thank you for all the things you have done
Because to me and your family, without you
There would be no rising sun.
Love,

Chloe Rose (12)

The Old Grey Lady

Under dense lids my eyes opened
I had a feeling of foreboding
My bedroom was like a refrigerator
I was chilled to the bone
My rockin' chair rocked on its own
That's when I knew I wasn't alone

I saw an apparition dressed in white
Her fabric was from another time and place
She had long grey hair
She wore a smile on her earthenware face
She made her exodus before daylight

Slumber wouldn't come back to me
So I watched the rising sun
A new day has just begun
She only calls
When night-time falls

She brings our parallel worlds closer together
I wish I could set her free
So she can rest in peace for ever
Then she wouldn't have to disturb me

Was she really there?
Did my imagination get the better of me?
You sleep in that house if you dare
Then you will see.

Michael McNulty

Life Goes On

I cannot sleep at night for fear
Of every single lonely tear
Being heard or being seen
Flowing into a ravine
Of hopes and dreams disillusioned
Then poured into a mocking sky

The world moves on yet nothing new
Arises with the morning dew
The silent night, the roaring day
Leaf in autumn, lamb in May
All around the world moves on
Then a thought of hope appears

Born upon a midnight; silver
Gaze in wonder at the chilver
Could this creature of the light
Make it through its first cold night?
As the mother waits to see
The newest dawn approaches

Of everything I've said and done
I most failed my education
I sit at home, the volume low
These written words, my soul's echo
To smile again and be carefree
Is that too much to ask?

Dat Guy Dere

Security

Today I'm feeling so secure, as money in the bank
Tomorrow I'll be insecure and fear death, let's be frank
Next week I'll be secure, with good family and friends
Next month I'll be insecure, war news the TV sends
Next year I'll be secure, at work indispensable
Then I'll be fired and insecure, I should have been more sensible.

Mark Musgrave

Oarsman

Don't row a boat here alone at night
Though this lake appears a placid sight.
Suddenly, wide-awake,
An overgrown water snake
May thrust up its head all set to bite
A savage light glitters in its mesmerizing eye,
You cannot row further, though you try.
Pray hard to stay afloat
In a still upright boat.
Though that ghastly head blots out the sky
While it twists its neck from side to side,
Those gaping jaws leave you terrified.
Teeth jut out so jagged . . .
Hear your own breath rasp, ragged . . .
Left too late, rowing away to hide.
Now, monster snake coils ever greater,
Inside that mouth is a red crater -
For a whole navy room -
Inescapable doom -
For how can you reach some shore later?
Unless you hurl oars into that gap.
Wait until you hear those huge jaws snap -
Leap over the boat side
Before that snake can glide
After you - then swim without mishap.

Chris Creedon

Salvation In My Mind

So, you think you've found a saviour of your own?
First you find your heart, then you lose your soul.
The path that I travel, makes me feel so alone . . .
Hope I find my way, I just want to be back home.
So you think you've found, the thing that you call peace?
Standing at the end, waiting for the last release.
I try to spread my wings, because I think that I can fly,
The days just turn to years, as you see how time goes by.
I don't always understand, all that I need
Emotions steal the food, that my soul needs to feed.
So, you think you've finally found the end?
Condolences returned, from intentions that I send.
The light seems to collapse, to the demons of the night.
Hope and faith are vanquished, nothing left but fright.
Though the apple's quite rotten, you take another bite.
So, you think you've finally found yourself
Conveniently stored, on the back of some shelf?
When you gaze out, the reflection that you see,
Seals your fate, determines who you will be . . .
I see change, as it starts, yet stays the same,
You better wake up, it's your thirty seconds of fame.
So now you think, that you stand in the sun?
Nowhere left to turn, nowhere left to run.
The light shines down, chases away the night,
The future is upon me, the sun is shining bright . . .

Mark Russell

85

The Postman

'Twas the day after epiphany and all
Through the village - on this working day
Nothing was stirring - not even a sleigh.
Cold cinders lay in the hearth - no fires were glowing,
All the doors were locked, so he looked in the windows.
Letters lay unopened - in sack upon sack,
No snipping or sewing- no painting or *rat-a-tat-tat.*
The warehouse stood silent - amongst empty racks
Down at the stables in the lantern's glow
Reindeer lay all snuggled up, asleep in the hay
Then from the dormitories, carried on the wind came
A coughing and wheezing and plenty of sneezing.
There lay in row upon row of tiny beds,
Full to the brim with elves with feverish heads.
'Oh dear,' came a sigh, 'oh what can we do?'
Then came an idea, as bright as the moon,
From the trolls' cavern, deep underground,
Came barrel of barrel of moss-green soup.
'We'll give it a try, it's all we can do.' The idea was sound.
Then one by one each elf left their sickbed, none to soon,
And back to their work benches - double quick.
Carried on the winds comes whizzing and *rat-a-tat-tat,*
Now echoes happily across the valley.
The work was resumed - now everyone's better.

David Charles

Breda

An apparition at the door,
A face I had not met before,
So softly you spoke my name,
And although I was frightened,
You bathed me gently in my pain;
The night you walked again alone to Doolough
In the torrents of rain.

Sean Conway

Credit Crunch

Is it just within me, or a social hunch
That everyone now has hit the credit crunch?
Last year our town was striving
This year we are barely surviving
It's going to get a whole lot worse
Before it gets any better
Each morning I hate to receive the post
In case it's a final demand letter
Not just hitting our pockets
Also damaging our pride
As we delve deeper and deeper
Into this financial suicide
Stores were heaving at Christmas
As people used to predict
Now they are so empty
So alone and derelict
So many job losses and out on the streets
Using cheap shops just to be able to eat
When we had money and credit cards
There were so many happy places
Our kids still want the same
As we put on brave faces
The social hunch, or again, is it just me?
Live for the day when again we will be stress free

Daz Smith

Unwelcome Guest

An unwelcome guest
has graced
my waist.
All I ate
was chocolate,
but I did not
invite *the fat!*

Shilla Mutamba

87

Space

Every man needs a garage or shed
To get away from the woman he wed
A special place to call his own
Some private space to be alone
A room where he can go and be
Away from all the family
It doesn't need to be large or flash
No need to spend a load of cash
Something simple with a comfy seat
Where he can sit and rest his feet
And ponder on the day's events
You'll find he comes back less intense
Refreshed, relaxed and then what's more
Ready for whatever chore
For once he's had his time of rest
He'll return, so full of zest
You'll hardly recognise your man
So take heed of this simple plan
Just find your man a private zone
That special place to call his own
And once this need has been fulfilled
I'm sure you'll both be more than thrilled
A little distance, and private time
Will make your marriage most sublime.

John W Fenn

Our Village - Sutton At Hone

Our village is an interesting place
Its folk, benevolent and fair of face
The River Darent, ever cool
Delights us all as it flow through
With verdant fields, ever producing
God's good gifts, to us His children
St John's our church, inspiringly tall
Where Christians meet, inviting all
Crusader knights, home from the wars
Once stayed here to nurse their sores
St John's Jerusalem, they convalesced
Then in the chapel they were blessed
Our library, a hive of information
Cheerful staff, serve in dedication
The Greyhound pub with its olde worlde charm
With its welcoming meals, feels cosy and warm
Our children, future citizens all
Skip and laugh their way to school
The post office, a place for felicitations
To shop, to post letters to our beloved relations
With discos, quizzes and outings galore
There's plenty to do, nothing to bore
Young and old thrive side by side
In a community, so alive.

Wendy Andrews-Nevard

Five Minutes On A Cycle, But . . .

Elizabeth, village cleaning help, known to all indeed,
She'll do any job for you if ever you have need.
She knows the village happenings, each day she will add more,
To her information, believe me she has a store.
Where'er she goes she's greeted with hellos and happy smiles,
The times she's cycled round that patch must add into miles.
When she's time she'll cycle back to those who had gone out,
Knowing if she doesn't, they'll have *that* to moan about.
A call she does near village shops means she slips in for honey,
Doesn't want to spend too much, saves hard her meagre money
To buy her home, and with her husband make it how they like.
That's why doing paper rounds and other's housework won't
make Liz strike.
Some folk she helps to wash and dress, for others just housework.
Like or lump the people, you cannot a job shirk.
She wears long, warm training slacks to keep the breeze at bay,
Aided by an extra cardie if it's a colder day.
Boots will keep her feet warm when winter snow is here,
While trainers keep her feet just right when summer's sun appears.
Even in this year folk work as hard as hard can be,
Because when the land was doled out, some forgot to bend
their knee.
As Liz will tell you, gaining possessions means hard, hard work,
And like our village daily, no job can you shirk.

Barbara Goode

Life Is Like That!

To paint a pretty picture,
Take a page that's clean and white,
A bunch of many colours,
Mixing dark and light.
Now faintly with lead pencil
Depict a well-thought scene;
Then ask guidance from the heavens
To enhance your chosen scene.
Let your hues be complimentary;
Reflecting peace and light,
Add just a touch of drama
With the blackness of the night . . .
When at last your work is done
And closely you inspect,
Highlight all the good things . . .
Then all the rest . . . respect!
All life is like a painting,
Resplendent on the wall;
And we are all the colours,
Whether great or small!
Tho' 20 yeas have now passed by;
Yet still remain the same,
Life's many worded teachings
Shine from their golden frame!

P E Woodley

Castle College

(Xmas 2006, by a satisfied customer)

She's alright is Louise,
She's cutting my hair
In a dropped waist skirt
And her midriff bare,
With a little black cap
And a pearl in her hair,
She hasn't a care, Louise,
And I envy her.

What it is to be young,
Not to be in this chair,
To have long flowing locks
And plenty to wear.

To attract all the lads
Who glaze as they stare
Oh, I envy Louise,
I would like to be her.

Instead as I sit
We chat and we share,
Talk of this and of that,
Especially *hair!*

J Harrington

Robin . . .

There is a little robin
In my garden every morn,
He must be quite old
For he looks tattered and torn.
He gives a little chirp
When I approach with his feed,
My garden companion,
A lovely friend indeed.

Christa Todd

92

4-12-08

Another day begins with breakfast TV
An insight of news as it would be
Interest rates falling faster than light
Gas and electric reaching new heights
Shannon's mum is going down
An evil witch from a dirty town
She looked like the Devil but took no one in
How does a mother commit such a sin?

A girl was stabbed at least twenty times
A deadly reminder of our woeful times
God willing she survived and tells the tale
For her the news is a world that fails
And look now it's snowing, so shut all the schools
Daren't risk breaking health and safety rules

Oil's coming down faster than VAT
But it's a drop in the ocean to you and me
Spend, spend, spend is what they suggest
Even though they got us into this mess
So pick up the paper for cheerful news
Not a chance now they've banned cheap booze
Bring back closing time and give us a break
Wake up, Gordon, for everyone's sake

John Foster

Friendship

I've learned in life what friendship means,
A blessing, a diamond, so precious it seems.
To laugh along together, and sometimes share the tears.
Sharing our lives together, to reminisce the years.
To be blessed with a true friendship that is in your heart so true,
You will never feel lonely your whole life through.
So now I want to thank you, knowing that you are there,
To have someone to count on and feel you really care.

Karen Logan

Kissing Love

Under an autumn moon, I loved you.
As the moon caressed your face
I knew that warmth would stay forever,
Nothing could take its place.

I felt your heart beating softly,
Gazed at your beauty so divine,
I knew I would love you for evermore,
That your soul and your heart were mine.

We kissed, and the world was our oyster,
Your lips were so deliciously sweet,
I wanted to kiss you for ever then,
Kissing love, in love, not parting to eat.

Kissing unites souls, and tastes and lips.
Perfumes bound, soft breath on your face.
A serious yearning, an ecstatic heart.
No room for others in our intimate space.

My memories stay with me, always and ever.
The kissing stopped and my heart was alone.
Your gentle lips haunt me, regrets I have few,
We must renew our kissing love, or my heart
                                    will turn to stone.

Brian Hurll

Pass

'Would *you* ever?' she says, 'Would you?'
She chews her words like gum.

That bird's wing fluttering in his ribcage
guards his marriage like a fob.

Like the layer upon layer of a maryoshka
he blows her bubble.

Rosemary Benzing

94

Estuary

Lazy on the high grassy rise
Above the shoreline,
With pleasure gaze
On small yachts
Of the estuary yacht club
Riding at anchor
Straining at their mooring,
Bobbing on the high tide,
Gaze across-wise
At the opposite estuary shore
Of the wide
Estuary.

Mid-stream container ships
That are there,
In the deep water channel,
Sailing to and fro.
Upstream to an inland port,
Downstream towards the North Sea,
Distant lands, ports.
Sunshine reflects off the water
Reflecting the sheen of solar bright.
Lazy with pleasure and gaze at the estuary.

B G Clarke

Being Alone

The paths are long
The hills are steep
The skies foreboding
Our minds may weep

We are never meant to suffer
Sometimes we are meant to be alone

But our lives are at their most empty
When we choose to stay alone.

Mike Hynde

Gardens Of Babylon

Before you blossom the trees,
Where the honeysuckle grows;
Beside you dance the water lilies,
Upon the gentle stream flows;
Around you the fountain springs,
Play like an emerald harp;
Their lullabies surround you,
Offering pearls of love from the heart.

Above you the petals of tropical buds,
Fall incandescently in the breeze;
Below you shine upon the tips of the grass,
The dew of summer's dreams;
To you comes the harmony of nature,
The spirit of spring is calling;
From you emotions are expressed in your eyes,
Upon the petals, your soul is blooming.

With you is the bliss
Of the secret world's melody;
Inside you is the golden key
To enter this garden and within yourself,
Be free.

Ross Baker

Live And Let Live

Live and let live
The way our world should be
Freedom for you
Freedom for me
Freedom for all
Be you black
Be you white
Freedom for all
It's only right

Greeny62

My Gap Year

I'm going on a gap year
I've worked so long and hard
Spent long hours in the office
On so many boring jobs

I will go on safari
Climb snow-capped mountains high
Learn some scuba diving and
Maybe swim with sharks

I know about the dangers
Of drink and drugs and sex
No carrying strange packages
From someone I've just met

I'm going on my gap year
No need to make a fuss
This is the big adventure
I've always dreamed about

So smile and just be happy
And make your old gran proud
I just want for my retirement
The fun I never had

Rosemary Jennings

The Stag

An ancient stag
stands
in ancient lands,
with prongs for hands,
proud and free.
He's hunted with glee.
He hunts the hinds
with docile minds.
His horns are in the hunter's bag.

Keith Murdoch

My Simple Pleasure

I love my car. It is just what I need.
Down country lanes, I can take my ease.
But on motorways bold I enjoy the speed,
My happiest possession, it knows how to please.

I don't like the towns. Parking is a pest.
Busy streets and pedestrian crossings.
Quiet country lanes suit me the best,
No traffic wardens and their bossings.

A trip to Arnside. Oh heavenly joy.
That gorgeous lake, when the tide's full in.
And fish and chips, the best you can get,
Then country roads for an excellent spin.

Oh how I enjoyed that ride to Buttertubs Pass.
That wide open country was never better seen.
Drive down to Howes for a welcoming glass
And reflect on the wonderful sights I've seen.

I shudder to think that there will be one day,
My driving will come to its eventual end.
I will sit in my armchair and dream away,
Dreaming of the view just round the next bend.

Albert E Bird

Golden Advice

The sunlight paused between the trees today,
In patterned splendour there, as if to say,
'No locks, no barriers, hold my precious worth,
Gold for the taking, and, no purse.'
More faintly still, the breeze replied,
'Take all this treasure, in your heart to hide,
Lest trouble dark beside your path should stride,
Then you may pay with gold of Heaven's worth,
To purchase joyous laughter and deep mirth.'

Mary Hughes

Over The Rainbow

I'll meet you over the rainbow,
right beside the pot of gold,
the place where dreams come true
and where my story of love unfolds.

Over the rainbow, yes I'll meet you there,
'tis the most blessed place to be
we could dance our lives away
flying over the rainbow so free!

Where dreams are born and come true,
and wishes are pinned to angels' wings
this most wonderful and special place
filled with light and beautiful things.

Way past the heavens, paradise found,
above the seven wonders and the raging seas,
come soon my darling, don't make a sound
for I'll give you a new life and set you free!

Over the rainbow I stand for you alone,
beside the pot of gold I wait
for you, my love, this very night,
come quickly my darling, don't be late!

Simon Foderingham

Journey To The Sea

I travelled for miles to reach the sea,
One gorgeous sunny day,
The sea was calm and peaceful,
As I looked out across the bay,
Hoping to see my true love,
On that gorgeous sunny day,
But now I know it'll never be, as he was lost at sea,
I live in hope that he'll return,
On that calm and peaceful sea.

Amanda Beeby

Being Dead

What is the meaning of life
Does anyone actually know?
Can no one tell you how long you have
Or why time's going so slow?

When you leave this world
What happens to you then?
Is your life completely over
Or do you live again?

When you're laying in that wooden box
And your body's cold and grey
You find that Death has paid you a visit
And taken your soul away.

As the nails in the coffin begin to rot
And you're laying there all alone
The maggots start eating at your flesh
Until all that's left is bone.

A gravestone full of beautiful words
Always being read
Because everyone is still there for you
Even though you're dead.

Jade Bradley

'Twas Forty-Seven

With ev'ry gust of wind that blew,
The old shed creaked, and then let go,
As bits of corrugation flew -
And lay in tatters o'er the snow.

'Twas forty-seven as I recall,
It was a cold and fretful year,
When winter tossed a large snowball -
Wi' children laughing ear to ear.

More hostile than the guns of war,
It wrought the country to despair,
With icicles from Heav'n to floor -
With no one going anywhere.

Ah, I remember fondly now -
What stillness drowned the village street,
Upon each rooftop, bush and bough -
And underneath each other's feet.

I too remember how, long gone -
A corrugated rusty sledge,
Wi' ten of us all clinging on -
Went hurtling through a prickly hedge.

Derek Haskett-Jones

Chelsea Glory

It is the floral event of the year,
With royalty gracing the show.
The rich and famous have their day,
Plus the presence of gardeners 'In the know'.

Much work takes place prior to opening,
As each garden has a theme.
Builders, designers and gardeners,
Must work closely as a team.

The floral tent is heart stopping,
With flowers of every hue.
Old plants will be shown in fresh colours,
New varieties make their debut.

Attention is given to detail,
In every entry shown.
As judges and visitors
Will notice the product they have grown.

Success will be rewarded
To the best on every stand.
But remember flowers and produce,
Are formed by God's own hand.

F L Brain

Until . . .

Until we stop taking and learn how to give
There will never be peace in this land where we live
Until we stop killing others because of their race
And stop judging people by the colour of their face

Until we stop preaching religion and let people decide
What they want to believe in, faith should come from inside
Until we stop fighting wars which we really don't need
What we spend on war, the whole world we could feed

Until we remove poverty and start helping the poor
We must be less greedy and realise that less is more
Until we can live next to our neighbours without taking their lands
And realise the fate of this world lies in all of our hands

Until we can say hate is truly a thing of the past
Only then can the peace we seek possibly last
Until we can look deep into our hearts and find
Love and respect for the whole of mankind

So we must start planting seeds of peace all around
Until peace in this world is finally found
Because only then can we really begin to live
As we will have learned not to take, but to give.

Stella Mortazavi

Forest Dances

Around shapely limbs silver birches
flirt their skirts
to the sound of a fandango
The stately poplars bend their backs
and stiff knees
in a tango
Willow trees waltz long meadows
in their crinolines
And lumbering beeches juggle
squirrels with swift hands
While holly trees join merry circles,
dancing on Circassian sands.

Rowan trees, the mountain ash,
Barn dance to tunes by Johnny Cash;

While hornbeam, with the younger saplings,
Plays jazz until the welkin rings

And bracken, gorse and prickly brambles,
Make hay amid the trotting shambles.

Until the moon, worn thin with playing
Yawns, and puts the blues away.

Myra Ranger

Whit Sunday

In a rack and pinion chatterbox car -
Pulled on an iron slashed scar,
To the summit we squeal, man, woman and child -
Pentecost pilgrims bewitched and beguiled.

At journey's end by Blodwyn's Seat -
I track the work of rabbits' feet,
To hatch the whimsy of a plan -
To be the solitary man.

Unravelling like a mainspring thread -
Tightly wound inside my head,
My mind begins to justify -
Why men must walk and birds must fly.

Why bees and wasps and hornets sting -
And stones are set in fairy rings,
Why seagulls cut a washed blue sky -
Above a pea-green sea tureen.

Why brave men die whilst their women wait -
Why dreamers dream and hesitate,
And here in my eyrie of chiselled stone -
Why I feel this need to be alone.

Philip Mee

I Wish I Had A Way With Words

I wish I had a way with words
That nobody could deny,
I'd write of wondrous things I'd heard
And tragedies to make you cry.

The whisper of the wind in the trees,
A leaf swirled by the breeze,
Of all these things I'd love to write,
If words would come to me.

Sweet breath of bluebells in the wood
And azure skies above,
I'd like to write if I just could
About the world I love.

I'd write of swaying, golden corn,
Of bumblebees that hum,
The blood-red hue of poppy fields,
If only words would come.

A rainbow or of virgin snow,
The gambols of a lamb,
I'll write it all one day, I know,
I can, I can, I can.

P Penfold

Ladybird

A ladybird landed on me,
exploring through my hairs,
as I sat writing poetry,
recording old affairs,

and as I paused a little while,
to watch this 'bird explore,
I noticed ants and spiders I
had never seen before.

And wondered if like I, they had,
affairs creating pain,
or were their only worries known,
of mankind, food and rain.

I wondered if they knew of death,
or that they'd all be dead,
by time the oaks and elms were bare,
of orange-yellow-red!

In turn I thought of me, and mine,
and all this meant to me,
so told the ladybird to fly,
'Time's ticking don't you see!'

Sid 'de' Knees

My Nocturnal Friend

When sleep won't come you're always there
my guardian of the night,
With all my hopes and dreams laid bare
black becomes a soothing white.

My guardian of the night
I see you clearly in my mind.
Black becomes a soothing white
I hear your words - so calm, so kind.

I see you clearly in my mind.
Are you my parent or my child?
I hear your words - so calm so kind,
Your voice is soft - your touch is mild.

Are you my parent or my child,
My spiritual comfort and my friend?
You voice is soft - your touch is mild.
I could wish the night would never end.

My spiritual comfort and my friend;
With all my hopes and dreams laid bare
I could wish the night would never end,
For when sleep won't come - you're always there.

John Willmott

Peace, Walk With God

Earth, is the name of our planet,
Mother Earth, if she is called, by her name.
We are privileged, and honoured to be here,
Living proof, that life is not just a game.

Why are the people, unhappy?
What makes the violence erupt?
Killing each other, is not the solution,
Talk to each other, listen, take stock.

Surely, for all of the children,
Whose lives, are so precious and dear,
They are the people who matter,
Let them live, on this Earth without fear.

Why are people, dying of hunger?
What stops the food, getting through?
Feed the starving, the children, they are the future,
Give them hope, love and compassion, too.

Put an end, to the cruelty and suffering,
Unite, join hands, be as one.
Let peace be the answer for all men,
Walk with God, and let His will be done.

Shirley Thompson

Untitled

It is so lovely to write,
Words that enter your head,
Could be thoughts of the living,
Or thoughts of the dead.

Some make you laugh,
Then next you may cry,
All these things remind you
Of times that have gone by.

Your lives pass by quickly,
Through trouble and strife,
Just count your blessings,
Get on with your life.

Thank the Lord for each morning,
Say a prayer every night,
With faith in your heart,
You'll find things turn out right.

So please pray for others,
Then you will find,
The best gift from Heaven,
When you learn to be kind.

Carol Elsmore

Metal Bird

The big metal bird hovered on high,
Like a great golden eagle in the sky.
Hovering and swooping, flying so low,
Trying to find those men down below.

Those mountainous waves rose fifty feet high,
As if trying to pluck the big bird from the sky.
'There's some men over there,' the pilot did shout,
'Quick, lower the winch and let's pull them out.'

Sweeping and swooping over the mountainous waves,
The Sergeant kept plucking men from watery graves.
That's all of them out, isn't it great,
But for one brave soul rescue's too late.

Those who were rescued were carried shoulder high
Sailors saved by men from the sky.
But for one brave soul whose life was all spent,
Nothing for him but a Bosun's lament.

'There's still men out there,' a sailor cried,
'If it wasn't for you we too would have died.'
Now the sky is all black and covered with cloud,
For those men still out there, the sea is their shroud.

Ronnie Shaw

Many Days

There are days like today
When the world can be unkind
The sky casts a cloak of misery
Sadness fills the mind

There are days like tomorrow
When the cloudy mist may lift
Sun shines to light a tired soul
Its warmth a welcome gift

There are days like yesterday
If I had only known
That yesterday's tomorrow
Would only make me groan

There are days yet to experience
Who knows what they will bring
A sense of satisfaction
That will make the spirit sing

Every day is precious
Hold it tight within your hand
Smile and laugh, enjoy yourself
We are but once upon this land

Lynn Elizabeth Noone

Time To Dream

How is it that as life departs
And memories measured distance grows
A softer sepia picture starts
To colour all, as a faded rose?

Neglected thoughts swim in the eye
The inner one not shown to another
They search about, bringing tear and sigh
For those left behind, time cannot recover

Like puppets on a carousel
Joy, pain and hope all circle through
The show goes on, it will not dwell
On the flickering moments that once you knew

There is no reason to sidetrack
From the path that leads to Heaven's door
We're made to cycle, for at our back
Our sons are sowing next season's store

Dear friends, take comfort from this thought
On leaving this life we've grown to love
Regret those cruel deeds, for which we were never caught
And pray for those left, from somewhere above.

Charles Keeble

Oh Lady

The last time I saw you
in that wee tartan shawl
your bright eyes were shut
though they did open once more

As I patted your head
for the very last time
the tears from my eyes
they did fall to the floor

You lay there so still
no breathing at all
your body was broken
you had taken the fall

My wife stood beside me
her tears they did swell
your wee friends at home
we yet still have to tell

Your pain it is over
you took your last sigh
dear lady you've left us
for the home in the sky

George Bremner

Paramedic

Sirens sounding
Blue lights flashing
Hearts are pounding
Quickly dashing

Life or death
Who can tell?
Take one last breath
And say farewell

A dreadful day
The mother crying

'Please stay, please stay'
The child is dying

An ambulance arrives
The crew is here
They're saving lives
And calming fear

The shift is over
The mood is light
Until they face
Another night.

Debra Webb

One Person's Protest?

Passive smoking is considered objectionable,
'Quite rightly,' many will say.
And what of those folk, who think it's a joke,
to throw litter and then walk away?

Well, I have my own little protest,
it is about the misuse of the tongue,
Foul language I am told is accepted as normal,
be you rich, poor or older or young.

I once made the mistake of requesting,
'Would you please from foul language refrain,'
There's no need to describe the reaction,
suffice to say never again.

If it's not fair that I breathe in your cigarette smoke,
if it's illegal to discard your refuse,
Then why is it right to make an assault on my ears
with a torrent of verbal abuse?

It seems things can't get any better, as
I watch parents swear to their child's face,
They will just follow the mould of bad speech,
till its hold, is a blight on the whole human race.

Eileen Wilby

Reality, Not Dreams

Life could be so simple
If we could only see
The things we see around us
All are given free

The trees with their sweet blossoms
The blue skies and the sun
The rivers and the wildlife
Nothing bad, there's none

Walking country lanes and mountains
Birdsong that fills the air
Things that are given freely
We forget that they are there

Sometimes we're so busy
Collecting material things
Things that rot and fall apart
That briefly make the heart sing

The difference is in nature
The ever-changing scene
Always gives you pleasure
Reality, not dreams

B Page

Whispering Lunar Incantations

I touched forbiddenness
twice tonight . . .
The woolly wreaths wore away
till a deep delight grew and lay
filling itself
drip-drop-drip . . .
as I walked with a wine-red me
by my side.
The acts smelt of a livid swoon
through the lips
of the purple moon
my eyes . . .
clasped on like a vice
to the sight
of me dipping further deep
a freefastfluttering veinless leaf
into a feel that stirred so sweet
into the moments' mighty beats
across the lamplightkissed streets . . .
criss-crossing that which breathes beneath.

I touched forbiddenness twice tonight . . .

Avishek Parui

Misery

Rain! What happened to pathetic fallacy?
The sunlight falls on the tears streaming down my cheek
And yet the world keeps walking on by,
As if to seek a happier face to look upon.

It's you. You're standing there amongst the crowd.
Amongst the throng of people adorning the day
With smiles. It might be too difficult for you to say
What you really mean or want

To a person who cries.

Caroline Foster

117

Nature's Trap

December 2005, Western Australia
I feel lightheaded when my girl is near,
Her presence in this world is very dear,
She lightens my burdens if I'm feeling low,
With her, all my life I want to go.

Her smile, her charm, makes every day right,
She lightens my world, her smiling eyes bright,
In her presence I want to be,
Together in our world, creatively.

Big sparkling eyes, with a radiant smile,
My admiration she claims, all the while,
Without each other, our days are grey,
Togetherness is the only way!

Our time together passes too fast,
We will build our nest strongly, to last,
This meaningful world has meant it to be,
We remain together, for eternity.
Footnote:
*Our world is so in need of love; if it doesn't happen soon, it will be goodbye
civilisation!*

Alister Wilson

Dream Master

Taking hold of my thoughts as I venture to sleep,
making me happy, then making me weep,
causing me pleasure and causing me pain,
now I am frightened, alone again.
Letting me realise just what hurt means,
longing to have you share in my dreams.
Surging my feelings in joyous flight,
comforting me through the long dark night.
Waking then, in the light of dawn,
searching Dream Master, alas, you are gone.

Katrina M Anderson

Limericks To Make You Smile

There was a young man from Ukraine
Who went for a walk in the rain
He slipped up and fell
Straight into a well
And never went walking again.

There was a young woman from France
Who thought she would go to a dance
But her feet got so sore
That she fell on the floor
And was carried home in a trance.

There was an old man with a hump
Who taught his small dog how to jump
But the dog jumped too high
Right up to the sky
And came down to Earth with a bump.

There was a young lad from Bombay
Who always had plenty to say
He was drinking his tea
When he swallowed a bee
And was silent the rest of the day.

Denise Castellani

My Dream Of Dreams

My dream of dreams is to be a famous poet,
To travel the world, for a chance to show it.
I'd shake the hand to make this dream deal
What I'd give to make this dream real.
If I have talent, let it come through,
'Cause I really don't know what else I could do.
It's my true passion and hello, I'm Bobby,
I want this to be more than just a hobby.
I hope and pray that my dream will come true
'Cause I believe in myself, and that's nothing new.

Bobby Rainsbury

Hypnotic Moon

Hypnotic moon who casts your shadow
Across the plains of Babylon
To bathe its beauty in your silver glow
And then across the frozen Arctic wastes
To create a dream-like marble landscape

Hypnotic moon who leaves a silver pathway
Across the rolling oceans deep
Where white horses ride the crests of waves
And then across the black lagoon in deepest Africa
To force back the hunter's prowling eyes

Hypnotic moon who moves the tides
Across the shallows of the beach
To lap against the palm trees' feet
And then to rise and fill the ports
To free the tethered ships upon the sea

Hypnotic moon who radiates a misty glow
Across the rose gardens scented mall
To watch the lovers kiss and swoon
And then across the sleeping child
To bathe the dreams of innocents in ethereal light

D M Walford

Late Snow Of Spring

Blackbirds chirp through the garden
In search for bread or seeds
Black feathers, yellow beak
Stark contrast with the white carpet
Lying beneath their feet
Spring lambs undaunted by the chill
Skipping, playing and bounding
Over the white, snow-capped hill

Softness, quietness, lightness
Spring's white blanket spread
In a glistening whiteness

Over hills, plains and dales
Daffodils weary and frail, sagging listless
With spring's white burden of frozen hail

Shimmering, glimmering, whiteness
Glistening in the sun; they bring
Bright contrast with the green spring
Changing seasons with joy or sorrow
Pass away like the white snow
The very late snow of spring

Victorine Lejeune-Stubbs

Cosmic Crisis

In the outer atmosphere,
Explosion in the night.
A star blast, yes a meteor
That's how we see its flight.

It's drifting through the atmosphere,
Floating midst the sky,
But it's a crisis in the cosmos
And it's set the night on fire!

There's a crisis in the cosmos,
But we're living down on Earth,
There's a crisis in the cosmos,
It's just another human birth.

The cosmos is in confusion,
Yet the Earth it claims no strife,
Every man dependent on an inspirational life.

The Martians are revolting,
We humans simply saints,
Concerned with daily living,
Our attitude life taints.

Chris Norton

Container Gardening

Container gardening seems to be
The job most suitable for me.
Instead of vast potato plots,
Much easier to pop spuds into pots.
And flowers? Seek a friend and ask his
Advice on plants for hanging baskets.
One could go on till further orders,
Like banning work on flower borders.
Yes, containers, pots and tubs - indeed,
No mowing or unsightly weed.
Just flowers, packed from hedge to hedge
(And out of sight, one row of veg.)
Yet, before I start an idle laze
Recalling digging, hoeing days,
I'm so relaxed, stretched out to doze
I must turn on the garden hose.
All this watering, here's the rub,
For every single pot and tub -
Alas! The water's off! Methinks
I've nothing left to mix my drinks!

Ian Pulford

Untitled

The recession is on its way
Jobs dwindle and fray
Bills and mortgages fall through the door
Final reminders stare up from the floor
Off to get food for the table
Scour the aisle for the cheap label
Hats and jumpers to keep warm
Through winter's coming storm
No help from the banks
We will take your house, thanks.

S Davies

This Night

I am so tired,
Yet I cannot sleep.
I am so sad,
But I cannot weep.
Emotions and thoughts
Racing through my mind,
Searching for answers
Which I cannot find.
The ticking clock
That passes time,
Pen to paper,
Thoughts to rhyme.
The wind sounds angry
As I lay in my bed,
It will soon be morning,
Need to rest my head.
The flickering light
From the lamp close by,
Why can't I sleep?
Oh why, oh why?

J L Rimmer

22nd October 2008

What can be rummer
Than a year with no summer?
There's nothing to cheer
Winter's come early this year.
With snow in October
When driving, be sober.
It isn't December
Not even November
But there's snow on the ground
For us all to confound.

Catherine Blackett

The Begotten

I am the begotten, a being without birth,
I remain invisible whilst I exist on Earth,
I am neither he, nor she, I am made up of sin.
Do not think you can defeat me, for you can never win.
When God created the Earth, the sun, the moon
And all the planets known to Man.
I am the begotten, I am here to torment,
Ever since this world began.
Diseases and disasters are fashioned in my name
For I am the begotten, with eyes of fire and flame.
If you look you will never find me, for I am never there,
I am invisible, and for you I have no care.
I am all the sins of man and becoming stronger every day,
I control the weather, earthquakes and the rain,
I can also make you suffer, for I am the bringer of pain.
The more you sin, the stronger I will be.
Sinners, you will never hear the last of me.
I am, after all, the begotten. I take your hate, I take
                    your sins and multiply the cost.
So come to me, you sinners, your God counts you as lost.

James Ayrey

Postman Durst

There once was a man named Mr Durst
He had an odd way of quenching his thirst
Mr Durst could not function without a pint or two or three or four
Round about number eleven he had fallen to the floor
His remedy for a hangover was quite easy
Drink a triple whisky followed by a martini

Mr Durst should know better than to drink and cycle
But he has compartments to store liquor on his bicycle
He often delivers the wrong post to the wrong houses
Because he takes sips from the rum he keeps hidden in his trousers
Once someone sent a friend a bottle of champagne
The postman drank it and it made his legs go lame

If you hear a *hiccup* cycling down your street
It's probably postman Durst barely able to use his feet
If anyone who receives mail from Mr Durst
Could hand him an AA pamphlet
That would be more than greatly appreciated
Help him to turn wine into water
So his bar tab can become a whole lot shorter.

Samantha Carroll

To: The Cuttin' Room 2008!

Hi there folks, do you like my style?
Why not pop in and rest awhile?
Yes, come on in, and take a look
At all the styles in this here book.

Here's Tom - he's like a cockatoo,
And Jinny - well she's rather blue!
Here's Dick - he's going out tonight
Oops - his is a shade too light!

And Lily - oh ain't she a dream,
But when she's wed, she'll be all cream.
While Harry - is just straight and black!
If folk see him, they won't come back.

But Rose - she is the best of all,
With ginger locks, she's very tall.
She sparkles like a Christmas tree,
So long folks, from Granny B.

Oh dearie me, I near forgot . . .
The three who dress our hair a lot!

Beth Stewart

Derry (The Walls)

A long way from home,
Tall green oaks, the bog,
Kept out by the walls.

By the sea, a room at the top,
No ocean view, held in by the walls.

The goddamned walls, get higher and higher,
No sad songs, no dark music.

Cold pang of hunger,
Blue burning for home,
Derry-free.

An image still, a long time ago,
Clear waters, ocean green,
The lady, loved so well.

The walls fall, brick by brick,
Step by step, tall green oaks,
The bog, the smell of home.

The wrong side of the walls.

D Caomhanach

Vultures With Human Eyes

Looking out from my 6th storey window, day break
misery is in the air, and it takes me by the throat
clutching at my windpipe, I begin to wake
the wood separates and I take out my coat.

A quick glance at failure, looming back at me with weary eyes,
my hands caress the banister, as my feet meet the stairs
illumination, a flickering light greets me, surrounded by flies
a twist of steel, and I've never been so discontent, with just being seated in
a chair.

A quick yank at the nylon, and it clicks into place
my eyes meet the wing mirror, and motion begins,
concrete and steel guides to the corporate wasteland, commencing search
for a space
surrounded by vultures, with greased hair and seedy grins.

Motion has stopped now, how I wish it would start again,
the leather meets my unloving grip, as I'm ushered into my 9 hour grave.
Placing down my briefcase, I disengage my brain.
I wasn't born to be a computer: my freedom I crave.

Edward Spiers

Love

The more we love,
   The more we find
That God is good
   And friends are kind.
The more of things
   That we all share,
The more we find
   We have to spare,
For it is in what
   We give away,
Enriches us from
   Day to day.

Angela Rose Elizabeth Davis

On The Road

I often wonder what my dad would say
So many cars on a motorway
A man of sport, in so many ways
He loved the thrills up and down
On the Scottish hills

He would have fun with the cars today
Sporty and light, shiny and bright
All sizes and styles, a joy to see
Lining up for the Grand Prix

The days have long gone
When you could park with ease
Everywhere you go, it's a really tight squeeze
So many cars, not enough space
It really is quite a disgrace

So many need their cars today
They have often to go a very long way
And to get there and find no place to park
It really makes one feel quite mad.

Catherine Wigglesworth

Planet Earth

Ice melts and sea levels rise,
rainforest destruction as the desert fries.
Modern farming and habitat laid waste,
it surely is a human disgrace.
Superstore excess driven by greed,
a supply of local produce is what we need.
Carbon emissions and oil is king,
renewable energy is what we should sing.
The land where we live is only to rent,
it's borrowed from our children to whom it is sent.
We have a home, it's called planet Earth,
it's about time we realised what it's worth.

Neil Turner

The Gentle Breeze

A gentle breeze caressed me
It taught me how to live
A gentle breeze possessed me
Then taught me how to give
Through the good and bad times
I felt it on my skin
A cool and soft reminder of feelings deep within
This breeze will blow forever
I feel it all the time
Sometimes with too much pressure
For a sad and troubled mind
Yet if I refuse to catch it
If I cease to feel its force
I know that it will kill me
My life won't run its course
I felt the need to write this
There are things you have to do
So I'll finish with a gentle kiss
The gentle breeze is you

Philip Hutson

Friendship

When things in life bring you down,
When upon your face you wear a frown,
When times are difficult and you feel you can't see,
I want you to remember you'll always have me.
Life is crazy, fun and mad . . .
Things that happen can turn out bad.
Sometimes in life it's hard to cope,
This is a message to give you hope,
For you, my friend, are a special kind,
The special type that's hard to find.
I want you to know that wherever you are,
My heart is close whenever I'm far.

Lindsey Nicole Hazle

130

Book Mate Sue

Along my poetic path
I have journeyed so far,
Forty odd years of travelling,
It's been such a blast.
I am an international poet
And the fun is so fast,
Within my numerous anthologies
And magazines so free,
My name is often lonesome
With no one to talk to me,
It's a rare thing and an honour
To see the same names in other books,
Susan Mullinger, though, is different,
For she is often there too,
Say hello and how are you
So this poem is just for Sue,
My name mate,
My book mate,
I am glad I met you.

Carolie Cole Pemberton

Shadow Power

Some words and phrases just seem to flow,
But where they come from you do not know.
Always seeming to fall into place,
Inspiration received by you in good grace
And recorded with no effort on your part,
Words seem to flow from within your heart.
Your head drawing inspirational thoughts away
Those completed themes awaiting their day,
Discovering non-stop power working there,
Leading to a window of grateful prayer
For prompting a completely satisfying feeling,
Release reaching to the height of the ceiling.

Betty Bukall

What Is A Friend?

A true friend is someone who is always there;
When you have a problem, they're willing to share.

A true friend is someone who freely gives more than they take;
They pick up the pieces when they hear your heartbreak.

A true friend is someone who will put you first;
They cope with your lows, even at their worst.

A true friend is someone in whom you can trust;
An important trait, for me it's a must!

A true friend is someone who can come in all shapes and sizes;
They dare to bare all, they wear no disguises.

A true friend is someone who is all this and more;
Who always has a smile for you when you knock at their door.

A true friend is someone it sounds cliché to describe;
With whom there is a connection, an almost spiritual vibe.

A true friend is someone who always comes through;
My true friend is someone I have found in you.

Robert Shorey

Sarn Badrig Holiday Home

Little house nestled there
Built with love and so much care
Many feet have passed your door
Some to come, some before
Upon God's hillside is your home
Where beasts and birds freely roam
Safe within your walls we feel
Away from hurt and life that's real
True contentment for rich or poor
God's love awaits you at the door
To sea or mountains each may roam
But know for sure here is home

Susan Roffey

English Riviera Tour

Paul our coachman who drives with flair,
Breaking for a rest by Sidmouth's sea,
Carefully drove us to Torquay
And Livermead House Hotel's care
For our English Riviera tour
Along Devon's shores and through Dartmoor.

At our magnificent venue
We ate from a first class menu
Starters, soups, sorbets, main dishes;
Each chef fresh made from greens, fishes,
Fungi, seafood, cheese, game and meats
Crowned by countless tasty sweets.

As promised we saw great sights
Ate great meals and had comfy nights.
So farewell quick to please staff
And Paul always game for a laugh.
And thank you, Tim Rew and fine crew
And Woods for making dreams come true.

Ronald Rodger Caseby

I Wonder Why

I wonder why the sky is blue,
I wonder why the sun has a hazy hue,
I wonder why there's dark and light,
I wonder why there's day and night,
I wonder why it rains or snows,
I wonder why we wear clothes,
I wonder why we are black or white,
I wonder why stars shine at night,
I wonder why there are boats and planes,
I wonder why there are cars and trains.
Does anyone know the answers please?
If so, put my mind at ease.

E Riggott

133

Green-Eyed Man

Play your songs again, make me cry
I want to sink into your sea-green eyes
Your voice that sets my heart aflame
I shiver when I hear your name

Your vocal chords stretch like a cat
Take me from here, to where you're at
I feel the hairs on my neck begin to rise
I'm lost in the depths of green-sea eyes

There are stars in the sky straining to hear
The sweet sound of a song so pure and clear
My arms are inviting you close, to stay
To gaze upon you for one more day

I am the audience, bow to my applause
Whatever I am, I'm sure I am yours
Green-eyed man sing me your song
And bring me home to you where I belong

In your arms where I belong

Nikky Braithwaite

Poetry Stew

Take a cupful of words
and simmer on a stove,
add three pinches
of Barnsley, Hereford
and Hove,

Take a sentence, dice
and chop,
sprinkle in a comma
and full stop.

Take four capital letters
and thinly slice,
add to the words
to make *nice*.

Stir in rhymes one
or two, and
you've made poetry
stew.

Francis Page

For JT

A difficult one! How long is anon?
No - no need to know it
the length of an unknown poet.
It's the adverb I mean. Of dictionaries seen
Nuttalls, revised by the Reverend James Wood
I don't take to be very good
He says, 'Immediately thereupon' and 'soon thereafter'.
Chambers Twentieth Century - with illustrations,
Says, 'Immediately' and again deserves my remonstrations.
Even The Concise Oxford, I am sorry to relate
Says 'Soon' and 'presently' and though I hesitate
Perhaps I'm wrong and the word was not 'anon'
But 'I'll phone you. So long.'

Pauline Smithson

Goodnight - God Bless

Our Leo could never talk, stand or walk a mile
But he could break a million hearts with his beautiful smile
A more contented boy you would never meet
God gave him a heart in place of his feet

With his eyes he would often jest
If only he knew how many lives he blessed
The pain of losing him we cannot hide
He filled our hearts with so much pride
We were given a special gift to treasure
And his memory will live on forever

He was given to us for some twenty-five years
And he made them some of the best
But now we have to wipe our tears
And give our Leo a rest

We know you will suffer no more
Goodnight, darling
You made our lives worth living for

Simone Fontana

An English Ode

For England hath me in her arms,
succumb does a man to her many charms.
Able in ways to make me wonder,
each setting sun I grow fonder and fonder.
A strata of splendour maketh scenes enrapture,
holding your heart in perpetual capture.
No dimming light could ever find sweet repose
or any such abode, everlasting, clasping is a lantern
of light even when day turneth to night: the heavens requite.
I should not be replete but rather always receiving at
the paragon in which she is achieving: England's meaning,
to bestow and show beauty munificently
is and eternally will be an 'English duty'.

Matthew R Wright

My Onerous Dream

One night I dreamt I'd lost my comb,
And though I'd had another one
In the pocket of my robe,
But when I looked, it too, was gone.

I searched all round in every room,
High on the roof, deep in the lawn,
I rummaged drawers indoors till dawn.
(Would someone please invent a probe
for finding buried nylon?)

I rang my brother on the phone -
A policeman out in Washington -
To tell him of my missing comb
And of my endless goings-on.

In his calm and sober tone
He said, 'You need a comb, and not a gun.'
From miles across the globe,
He said, 'You could go buy another one.'

Mark VanWarmer

Me And My Dogs

Walking through gates and climbing over styles,
Me and my dogs will walk for miles,
Watching the rabbits scattering along,
Jumping and playing in fields so long.
Pigeons cooing, magpies nattering,
As I walk through lanes of old,
Me and my dogs stroll along.
Hills so long, trees so tall,
Mountains so high, lanes so long,
Me and my dogs walk them all.
The sunrise falling, the nights are drawing,
The crows are calling, the trees are blowing
As we make our way home.

Dean Howells

The Salt Of The Earth

Young or old alike, built in the same earth prototype,
In an endless quest for love and light,
Searching for ways to feather our nest,
To seize the day, longing for the best.

The crooked old woman was once
The Lady of the Ball- if she'd had the chance!
The blossom would've been soon of youth deprived.
Who's got any control on Future or his present life?

Her past could be only a twinkle away,
Her present becomes her past with this day.
Her blossom would have fallen on the ground.
It's the promising fruit in the tree that counts.

If at least once you have been told:
'You are the salt of the Earth
And the small light of the world',
No matter you're in your teens
Or at sunset, you've touched the horizon.

Cecilia Moldovan

Nonsense

Here is a little nonsense
Just a riddle to confound,
An archipelago of disjoint'd verse
Just syllables going round;

A moment like a mistim'd step
A convolution seemingly unsound,
A jumble and mishmash
That defies any logic to be found;

Praise me, for I keep this short
This fruit being blett'd until rott'n,
Clearly the oddest work I e'er writ
And so probably best forgott'n.

M Sam Dixon

Social Engineering

Social engineering started off with 'Do not smoke'
At first the people laughed awhile and took it as a joke,
Then, you might be too fat to sit upon that chair,
Maybe you should take off some weight, get slim like Tony Blair.
Try to eat a better diet, with some exercise and such,
Throw away that chocolate bar, you like it far too much.
When you appear on camera every time you have to shop,
For God's sake do not use your hood, you'll be shot by a cop . . .
Watch out for all those feral gangs of children on our streets,
Remember, when they menace you they'll ask for more
than sweets.
Do not touch the darlings, let them beat you half to death,
It's okay, there is no hangman now, waiting to catch their breath.
We did not ask them all to learn the humane texts of God,
So now they just lay on the ground, get drunk upon the sod.
These changes were all meant to be, the poor had grown too many,
So when they want to cull a few, who will be missed?
Not any.

Jean Paisley

Freedom, Love And Beauty

Freedom is the wet sand swaying between your toes,
The breeze on your shoulders and salt up your nose,
Your hair shimmering in the fiery skies,
On a day like this it will take you to new highs.

Love is the smile that plays across your lips,
And the new bounce in your shoulder and hips,
Unfazed and beautiful you now stand,
As the sunlight hits your face like a helping hand.

Beauty is my saviour and fills my soul,
A shiver runs down my spine and I feel a slight cold,
As I gaze out at the glorious, sandy beach,
The mysteries of life almost within reach.

Kimberly Harries

Love Is

Love is a thing you cannot hold,
It encompasses dreams untold,
A feeling of completeness,
An aura of happiness,
Love is missing you,
Love is kissing you,
Holding you,
Feeling you close,
Love is understanding you,
Enjoying you,
Running my fingers through your hair,
Seeing a smile being born from your face,
The sparkling of your eyes,
Love is walking together in the summer rain,
Love is profound,
Love is true,
But most of all,
Love is you.

Andy Powell

A Country Cottage

There's a cottage in the country
Where we spent many happy hours
Raising ducks, hens and geese
With a garden full of lovely flowers.

Two little dogs running around
As we pulled up the weeds.
Then, when spring came
We planted all the seeds.

The beauty all around us
Those peaceful, tranquil days
We will always remember
In our twilight days.

Julie Brown

Breakdown

I am still standing
After things I have seen
Feeling better now
Than I have ever been.
I have searched my soul
Broke free of my past
Discovering myself
At long last
Shed fears and anxieties

That for so long kept me down
Now swimming on the current
On which I always drowned
So here I stand
Tall and proud
Looking forward to a new tomorrow
I have brushed off all doubt and fears
No more sorrows do I have.

Donna Salisbury

Purrfect The Three-Legged Cat

Purrfect the three-legged cat,
A fine cat in every way.
Brown coat, brown eyes, three long gracious limbs,
She's lived with us for many a day.

She doesn't do much, just sits and watches
From her special perch way up high.
She refuses even to turn her head,
When a mouse goes scampering by.

She's quiet too and doesn't purr,
We really wish she would.
I'll tell you why she's so still and silent,
It's because she's made of wood.

Debbie Legall

The Flower Shed

There are flowers all around me
Beads shells crafty things as well
Baskets hanging from the roof
Not much room for myself

My mind is racing what will I make?
Arranging books by the score
I set myself so many tasks
I'd never get out the door

Beside the shed there is a tree
Blackbirds' nests every year
I leave my window open
To hear their chirpy cheer

It's so relaxing so peaceful
Working with flowers and cones
This little corner of the world
That I can call my own

Florrie MacGruer

Dream Weavers

A kaleidoscope of moving images
pours into my receptive mind;
every great song tells a story,
this is something I always find.

More than mere aural delights,
those lyrics to me are just like videos;
I close my eyes as my imagination takes hold
and enjoy my very own private shows.

I'm engrossed as the tales unfold,
the plotlines and characters seem so clear;
my favourites continue to give pleasure,
time after time and year after year.

I revel in the magic and wonder
which songwriters' creations can bring;
the world seems a much better place
when I hear the dream weavers sing.

Annabelle Tipper

Magical County

Cornish sunshine in December
Weather mild for time of year

Other places we remember
Where it could be cold and drear

Long the years that we have been here
Ne'er regretting that we came

Good and bad the times we've seen here
Still we love it just the same

All the time we've been perceiving
Sometimes sadness - sometimes mirth

Can't imagine ever leaving -
There's no better place on Earth!

Frances Coast

Looking Forward

Summer days have swiftly passed
The nights are drawing in again,
The leaves are falling thick and fast
Helped on their way by wind and rain.

All too soon, trees will be bare,
Standing like skeletons against the sky,
Shelter for birds, no longer there,
Piles of leaves by the roadside lie.

To wrap up warm against the cold
Is what we all must do,
Babies, toddlers, the young and old
Before we all turn blue.

We all will wish the time away
Until the start of spring again,
With skies no longer dark and grey,
And the sun to make us warm again.

Joan Corneby

Brush Strokes

The artist with his brush in hand
Observes his canvas on the stand
Ready to receive the coloured oils
Sweeping brush strokes from his toils
He ponders searching from his mind
A mental picture he must find
Creative colours yet to see
To be worthy of an artist's fee
Human, abstract or animal scene
Inspirations from a dream
With a painted picture now in mind
Full concentration he must find
Completion of all work to see
Determines worthy artist's fee

E L Hannan

The M1 Motorway

At the end of my garden, the motorway flows,
The traffic is endless as onward it goes,
It starts off at London, then goes through to Leeds,
Serving the public their travelling needs.

I watch out my window at cars speeding by,
The road once was fields, but hard as I try
To remember when concrete replaced all the grass,
The smell of fresh air, now replaced by the cars.

It's progress, they tell us, we need all this speed
To avoid all the towns, this is progress indeed,
We get on the motorway, foot to the floor,
The concrete snake takes us from door to door.

But before all the motorways came into play,
We'd visit more places, meet folk on the way,
We'd picnic in countryside, husband and wife,
The M1 is handy, but what cost to life?

Sandy Fryer

My Words

Words fail me when I look and see
A new dawn breaking out beyond the sea.
Words fail me when in spring the flowers appear
Daffodils, crocus, in beautiful colours bright and clear.
Words fail me when I watch a baby being born
And this happens daily, evening till dawn.
Words fail me as the killings go on daily
When each Christmas peace is spread yearly.
Words fail me when young ones are crying out
'Give us a job,' when leaving school they shout.
Words fail me as I see Christmas lights glow
I hope this world will get better, time will show.
Words I have plenty, now I'm getting old
So may my words remind you, you were told.

John Shanahan

Quiet Reflection

As I sit here in quiet reflection,
Dark winter has melted away,
It's spring again, new growth, new life,
My old friend died today,

In the midst of life's renewal,
Her golden hair turning to grey,
She loved the flowers, and bird song so sweet
My old friend died today,

We'd chat and put the world right,
She loved to gently pray,
For the troubled world we live in,
My old friend died today,

She's spent her life in the service of God,
So these words I wanted to say,
I'll never forget you, goodnight and God bless,
My old friend died today.

Dorothy M Mitchell

A Time Of Summer

I look above me and see open sky,
A fluke there are no clouds to block the sun
That gazes down upon his bright young sty,
Which sets, sows and seeds the hot summer fun.
Birds twitter and babble as I lay down,
Stretched long on my bristly yet comfy grass,
Freely flutter and baffle, yet their sound
Is a song for kids and grown-ups en masse.
Utopia, paradise, has smothered
The scary spectres of my modern life,
Stifled them, slammed the dice, has them cornered,
No need to be bothered with gun and knife.
But this divine bliss must end, I wonder why
I cannot be part of the open sky.

Joe Riley

146

My Uncle's Dunkirk

In fear and shock on this Dunkirk beach
Hosts of small boats trying to reach
These stricken, tired, beleaguered forces
Relentlessly strafed without any resources

Struggling to board these meagre craft
My uncle pulled on board with a laugh
He had a banjo clutched to his chest
A ray of hope in this whole bloody mess

He played them home with death all around
They made a most incredible sound
As the English coast came into view
The boatload were singing along with the crew

It's amazing how the human spirit responds
How a banjo and singing inextricably bonds
Men plucked from a hell of a beach and sea
Then welcomed home with a bun and some tea.

Len Peach

I'm Only Two

All the lifting and carrying I can cope with all that
I used to be bothered but now it's old hat
I still struggle with chairs, keep off tables and such
But they tell me that's okay so I don't care too much
So I stand here and wait and do as I'm told
Well you have to, don't you, when you're not very old
I fell down one day and my knee was all blue
But this happens a lot when you're a boy aged just two
Cos I keep telling my mum and sometimes my dad
That I'm only exploring and that's really not bad
For I'm testing myself and keep stretching far out
And I'm testing my voice as I try hard to shout
So when strange noises come clearly right out of the blue
Remember it's me and I'm still only two

Brian J Meehan

Twilight

The look in your eyes,
I'm terrified,
I can't release your hand.

Just hold me safe
And keep me warm,
Keep my feet upon the ground.

Your cold, pale skin
Against mine,
Sends shivers down my spine.
But your cold, pale eyes
Warm me up inside,
You'll always be mine.

You can tell when they're coming,
Just read their thoughts inside.
We can't keep on running,
Forever will we hide.

Natasha Bowerman

Invasion

Sea was vibrant green on the horizon,
Vanished in the distance flowed on and on.
Love walking on beach at this time of year,
Leave marks on wet sand, watch sea disappear.

Not for me the heat of summer season,
Torbay suffers a person invasion.
Winter is the time to go for a walk,
Hold hands with my spouse, as we stroll, we talk.

Appreciate I'm lucky by seaside,
Again gaze at sea and incoming tide.
Beauty of area is all too plain to see,
All year round enjoyed by locals and me.

S Mullinger

The Grandchildren

We will bring you smiles
When you come to call,
And tell you what we're doing
When we meet you in the hall.

We will give you kisses
And a warm embrace,
And tell you where we're going,
And take you to the place.

We will give you laughter
At a nothing price.
Just ask some silly questions
And we'll give you answers nice.

And when you wave goodbye
Going down the drive,
We'll go and spend the cash you gave
And wait till you next arrive!

Simon Wilkins

The Path That Led To The House

The garden path weaved to the left
and occasionally to the right:
The branches groaned and sagged
swaying to different angles at night.

The path was soil and sediments of dust
with stones rounded and chipped:
I walked and felt the Earth sculpt
avoiding puddles in case I slipped.

Paws and feet were signed in routes
to search for food and a mate:
But I noticed the path was dead
beyond the rusted garden gate.

Gareth Culshaw

The Encounter

Madelaine, dear Madelaine
what did I see
when turning to find
you looking at me?

The face of a starlet
projected on screens,
the sweetness of crumbs
Proust dipped in his tea

Eight decades between us
yet wisdom is showing
untarnished by time
that registers a truth
only you can perceive

So what can you see
Madelaine, dear Madelaine
when looking at me?

Godfrey Dodds

150

The Ghost Of The Sailor's Soul

I remember a time a long time ago
The memories are still in my head
A journey took place through time and space
In an ancient world thought dead

People gathered round to hear the sound
Of the sailor on the shore
But now the boat drifts along the moat
And the sailor is no more

People came nearer to remember the hero
A possessed new soul up ahead
The journey ended not as intended
As the sailor ends up dead

But his soul lives on through years that have gone
His soul will never seize
Let the world live tall through the sailor's soul
And let the world forever be in peace

Matthew Griffin

Make Someone's Day!

Just a friendly smile
And an encouraging word;
Could be two of the best things
Someone has seen and heard.

Just a friendly greeting
And a heartfelt 'Hello';
Could lift someone up
Who may be feeling so low!

For a smile without charge
And an encouraging word without pay;
Could really make a difference
In someone's life today!

Ray Varley

Human Being Possessing

Coming to this world
Clothed in nothing more than skin
'Tis from this very moment
That the journey doth begin.

Tending to accumulate
This and that along the way
Only to discard them
At the moment of decay.

The worry and the fear
These things they always make
If only we could value less
And not accumulate.

A heaven here on Earth
We really could create
Within ourselves a balance
That nothing could negate.

Errol Kavan

The Stream

The stream, my friend,
My liquid gold,
Your froth of beer,
Your stories told.

Fills my head
With marching bands!
Your charging horse,
Your clap of hands.

Gone so quickly,
You never leave,
Cleanse me gently
As you weave . . .

Geoff Ward

Full Circle

When I was four and twenty,
My mother said to me,
'Slip into the kitchen, Son,
And make a pot of tea.'

When I was five and fifty,
My mother said to me,
'I think you are a bit too old now
To be sitting on my knee.'

When I was seven and seventy,
My mother said to me,
'Slip down to the shop, Son,
And we'll have fish and chips for tea.'

Now I am nine and ninety,
There is no one here but me,
So I'll slip into the kitchen
And make a pot of tea.

Don Antcliff

New Year's Eve

Loved ones gathered,
Auld Lang Syne,
Champagne and wine,
Celebrating festival time.

Looking forward,
First foot through the door,
But still old ghosts whisper of the past,
Of the year that went so fast.

Loved ones gathered,
Auld Lang Syne,
Champagne and wine,
Celebrating passing time.

Steve Hurley

Limbo

What, where? Who knows why?
So hard to watch her bravely try
To find and form the words that once
Would barely touch her tongue then fly

Her diary holds the key to what was once a busy mind,
The theatre, arts and literature, interests of every kind.
Gardening, shopping, lunch with friends; all clearly marked as done -
My name is featured on each page, yes each and every one.

The last few years have brought us both to a safe common ground;
Our mother/daughter niggles shed and caring friendship found.
In her strange world her quicksand mind has lost the recent past -
My face a distant memory - my features fading fast.

I ask and beg for a reply
As hours and days trudge blankly by,
Caught in a fog that does not lift
No answer, just this *why?*

Gaelyn Joliffe

He Comes As Friend

He comes as friend
So do not fear Him
Behind his eyes see Love
The secret of our longing.

His smile, a recognition
I know your hopes, your fears
My love has long sustained you
See now I dry your tears.

His arms outstretched in greeting
His face alight with Love
Too long postponed our meeting
Welcome to your home above.

John Cook

2008

Pam Ayres - for Poet Laureate,
Is what I'd like to see,
And with this rather jolly thought
I hope you might agree?

The humour of this lady
Is unique in every way,
As with eloquence - and tongue in cheek,
With words she loves to play!

Her poems all touch on daily life,
And are easily digested,
No flowery words or phrases;
Nuance oft detected!

With lilt in voice - and soft dialect too,
Pam is a national treasure,
So her appointment to this royal post
Will from now on be my bold endeavour!

Peter Mahoney

Television

Ye stand in the corner and reign supreme
A medium to hopes and dreams
Family business to me it seems
Estranged by those hopes and dreams.

The programs designed to impress and amuse
Thy subjects are enchanted
The children's questions pierce the hush
Their questions answered with *hush* or *shush*

The voice of wisdom falls by the way
The way of violence here holds sway
A weeping mother a weeping wife
A loved one taken in the midst of life

Aye thou high and mighty curse
What minds doth thou pollute
What influence sways the mass
What heartbreak has come to pass

John Morrison

Vinegar

I missed you this morning at breakfast,
I buttered your croissant and scone.
I forgot that you didn't like butter,
I forgot the fact that you're gone.

So what did she make you for breakfast?
What time did you crawl out of bed?
Where do you spend your lunch-hour?
Am I still stuck in your head?

I'm sorry for all my shortcomings,
I'm sorry for the sugarless tea.
I take mine with vinegar now
Because that's what you taste like to me.

Shane Telford

Our Way Forward

The change of the times
Is about to explode.
Proving it is the man,
Not the overcoat or robe!

United we all stand,
For Harmony and Peace.
Now one big family,
As opportunities increase!

With unity and determination,
A future for all, will be.
Through the challenges ahead,
Accept your responsibilities, and see!

By getting our act together,
The world storm will subside,
Progress and change will happen,
Unselfish love, no lies!

Ann Beard

My 25p Birthday Gift

I received twenty-five pence
For my 80th birthday today,
So I'll have to write to the government,
And here's what I'll say:

'Thank you for the money,
But what can I buy?
There's not enough for a tin of soup,
Or even a mince pie.

So I suppose there's only one thing
I will have to do,
Is add 2p to it for a stamp
To send this thank you note to you.'

Jean Hendrie

This Rainy Day

Today was very wet and cold,
Nipping fingers and biting toes.
Soaking each and every one,
Taking away all of our fun.

With coats right up to the neck,
We all tried our best to not get wet.
We stamped our feet and rubbed our hands,
In order that we could keep warm.

But still our fingers all turned blue,
And before we knew it we were
Soaked right through.
With water dripping from our coats.

We decided the only place for us,
Was to travel home on the first bus.
Where there would be a glowing fire,
And we could get dry and warm.

Pauline Uprichard

In Retrospect

When Earth was made and all its mixture done,
each continent fought to gain its place and
settle down. A leader rose and reigned upon
the lesser ones below, who raised a hand
and asked for help to grow as equal one.

Creator looked and saw what happened when
left alone these myriad creatures grew
some good and others not, called men
and women, and all their children too
and saw the urgent need to enlighten them.

He sadly wondered why these awkward few
who already thought they were the chosen
ones to rule without restraint and not eschew
their wanton ways. Yet these egocentric men
would have to learn that even just the few
are His creation's children too.

Peter Muirhead

My Poem For John

(With love from Heather xxx)

What it is to love,
Is like a warm blanket from above,
It fills our hearts with light
And makes life an easier plight.

Less we forget the times
When love abandoned us there,
Always remember to love
And always remember to care.

There is only one love in life,
Is the lesson we all should learn,
It makes the world a better place
For us to live upon.

Heather Campion

Rocket Science

Why not channel the world's have-nots
Into a series of equal space plots
Even the Chinese can now reach space
So why not harness the poor of each race
They could all earn useful bucks
Zooming around in rocket space trucks
Overnight we'd dispense with handouts and doles
They'd be usefully filling in all those black holes
There could also be a technical gang
Who could solve the riddle of the big bang
Perhaps they could alter Earth's rotten weather
No doubt by smashing some protons together
And they could be trained in interrogation
To be used in any alien location.
They might find how the world evolved
Then the theory of everything would be solved.

Colin Burnell

Mommy! Mommy!

The restless posterity busily swirls
Like the whirlwind on a lone shrub -
Oh, the frantic pursuit of aching hearts,
Aiming connection with a sentient hub?

A willing red heifer died in isolation,
An infinite offering for a stained breed;
Denying love secured daily purification;
Maternal grace an ever published creed.

Into the dreadful place of banishment
The lioness-hearted benevolence risks all;
Ashes and living water her remedial scent,
A complete restitution her earnest goal.

Mother-plighted charity
A grand display of the Almighty's delicacies.

Gilberto Dias

Isle Of Thanet

A woodpigeon calls some mornings,
Just as the dawn is breaking;
The gulls overhead, I wonder what's said,
But theirs is the sea and it's taking;
Daffodils begin to bloom in the gloom
Of seaside Rowena Court
And all along the coastline
Are features of the Cinque Ports;
To this Isle of Thanet,
A Shalottian lady espoused,
To a vehicle of poesy,
And a shroud of musical mystical sounds.
Nearby, Rossetti lies, in slumber
On an evening tide.
On sleepless nights, the stars are bright and out,
The moon is clear with me and no other about.

Joy Sheridan

The Change Of Life

The world is ever changing, I try to keep up with it all
New money, new measures and weights now
I'm lost at the market stall
With a sigh I remember the old days
Coal fires, home baking and love
We had all of these in abundance
Are they lost in these days of must have?
But the world has always been changing
We too were the young ones once
Did we honestly think of our parents
As traffic and flying advanced?
I think as we all grow older
And our memories are softened with age
We forget to embrace the future
As the book of life just turns one more page.

Milly Holme

Dear Mr Mole

Dear Mr Mole
Why do you dig
Such a very big hole
In which to sit
And devour the worms
Which fall from your sky?
I like to see you
But please pass on by
Cos you leave big hills
On my nice flat lawn.
If you start right now
You'll be finished by dawn
Then you'll see the sunrise
O'er the field next door
Where you'll find there are
Jucier worms - and more.

B Williams

Wedding Day

Just a little poem
To wish you on your way,
We hope you both
Have a very happy day.
A wedding is a special time
To say how much you care,
And a time for mums, to shed a little tear.
So join together happily
On this special day for you,
And may life always be happy,
And forever true.
So as the bells ring out
And the confetti flies away,
It will be the start
Of a brand new life and day.

Marion Lee

Bathtime

Bathtime is my idea of Heaven,
I always dream of exotic lands and I unwind,
The daily grime of everyday life is cleansed off me in an instant,
I'm at peace and so relaxed is my mind.
I always love to soak in a bathtub full of gigantic bubbles.
I submerge myself totally in bath salts and scented foam,
I drink a glass of wine on the odd occasion for pleasure,
I feel so refreshed, alive and at home.
On Mondays I sink into an 'Avon Soft Pink' bubble bath,
At the weekends Baddedas invigorates my soul,
Radox has a hypnotic and sensational effect upon me,
Fenjal Crème Baths make me spiritually whole.
Bathtime is so wonderfully special to me,
I can spend quality time on my own,
Sometimes I do the Times Crossword in my tub,
Or chat merrily to my friends on the phone.

Fine Buliciri

Don't Look In, Look Out

Don't look in, look out!
Have no fears or worries
Just look out and shout!

'Now that I'm married
And have a beautiful wife
My life is now worth living
No hardship, trouble or strife.'

You see, love takes all the pain away
Which we suffer
From day to day, to day,
And comforts all the troubles
Which otherwise would be tough
And stops us hanging hat up
And saying, 'I've had enough!'

C O Schou

163

Beckoning

Come in the stillness
In the quiet of night,
Come in the dawning
Of morning light!
Beckoning, beckoning,
Calling to me,
Come blessed Saviour,
From sin set me free!
I've oft' missed your calling
As you stopped at my door,
Just come one more time
Don't pass me no more!
I want to walk with you,
Along Salvation way,
Call on me Jesus,
I'll come now, today!

Isaac Smith

Coffee Cup Sonnetina

I need another cup; I've more to write.
I head back in, turn back to get the cup;
The papers underneath it lift for flight.
I move them and I pick my pen back up.
Inside the house I switch the kettle on
And take the coffee from within the freezer;
I seek the cup to rest the cone thereon.
It's still outside, your Lord's name swearword geezer.

I go to get it and I bring it back.
Routine takes over as I wonder why.
I spill none as I tread the beaten track,
And then it hits me, there's no short supply!
But instantly, rejoinder conjures up
A patio full of each and every cup.

David Walmsley

Silly Isles

Had I a desert island
I'd rather it were two,
Or three so one could be my land
With two for me and you.
But four would be a better turn
For then we'd have one spare
And five would make a nice pattern
When seeing it from the air.
Now six would be an archipelago
And surely of the best,
While seven gives us one to sell
So we could keep the rest.
But eight would be too much to cope
So I just have to say
In such a crowd I'd live in hope
That we could sail away.

Nicholas Taylor

No Difference

For the quality not quantity
You're drawn to read all you see
With a chance to show my word ability
I will leave you breathless you will see
With words that are priceless and universal
With no repeat, omnibus or rehearsal
An original pattern of words that I wonder
Will organize unplotted and work with no blunder
A decoration of ideas laid flat out with emotion
Spare a thought for the poet's devotion
But whether spoke, sung or shouted
My words be free and ousted
And shared with all or kept to one side
It's no difference to me, I still have my pride!

Stuart Pickup

Eloise

She was as beautiful as a rose,
Yet her stare was as cold as ice.
A single word could leave you dead,
You'd never get near her twice.
Her hair was the colour of golden corn,
Her eyes like diamonds of blue.
A passionate heart beat deep inside,
Yet she was incapable of being true.
She'd win your heart with just a smile,
As her blood-red lips she'd purse.
You'll think it's heaven, but don't be fooled,
Her kiss is the Devil's curse.
Flawless skin of porcelain beige,
With nails like swords of steel.
A dream girl that could be yours,
But is she truly real?

Jan Garrod

No Care

A soul in abeyance
Upon the cusp of life
Awaits its eternity
Cruelty had been rife
No strength left for begging
Short rasps of bad air
No thoughts of anything
Does anybody care?
Darkness softly looming
The last slumber ensues
A soft, warm blanket of kindness
Halts our cruel, selfish views
No care in our community
No care in our schools
No care in our homes
We've broken all the rules.

Maureen Westwood O'Hara

River

A river flows serenely past a rest home to the sea;
My thoughts are as the ripples as they flow away from me.
My imagination haunting; I have many thoughts of life
And fondly in those ripples, I see She, my love in life.

In fancy are we walking beside this placid, peaceful stream
And her animated chatter holds me in a spell, as in a dream.
In my fantasy a lifetime passes, as walking hand in hand,
We see our memories on the ripples, carried to a Never Land.

As rivers run, so life goes on for those now left alone,
As the sea tide halts a river's flow, so age to us is prone
To stifle our exuberance; quell our hopes, to bring us fears;
But the river keeps on flowing and gently carries off our tears.

Patrick Glasson

Self Confidence

Self confidence, I often find
A trait unwise, too weak of mind;
Pure faith in one's ability
Belies words such as, cautiously;
And we all densely charge forth, blind!

The basic truth, not meant unkind,
Speaking as one of feeble mind;
Just watch the news each night,
And see self confidence!

Our fledgling race we call mankind,
Yet each an undeveloped mind;
A better world will someday be,
Respect for all, and dignity;
Maturity is but the key,
I've confidence!

Keith Miller

From The Sky

It falls,
Delicately on the earth,
A small piece of beauty
In this world unworthiness.
It does not deserve
What the sky has given.
A gift from above,
A message of love.

It melts,
The ground, hot with evil,
And it cannot cope
With this present from Heaven.
A smile from the sun,
Fills one man with glory,
One, who tells us this story.

Jessica Maxwell-Muller

Then The Moment's Gone

When the years go by so quickly
And some had many tears
The nights were oh so lonely
I forget then to count the years
When I walk in the darkness
The hills they seem to glow
When the moon shines on the valley
Deep and crisp with snow
Those days with you I remember
And counted one by one
Now as I grow older
I thank God for everyone

Doris Moore

Come Unto Me

Sophia, my love, come unto me,
Grant me your gnosis, enlighten me.
I stagger as blind, I can't see the way,
How long must I suffer? How hard must I pray?
Sophia, my love, come unto me,
Don't leave me in darkness, trapped in my clay,
Give me my freedom, open my heart,
Show me the daylight instead of the dark.
Sophia, my love, come unto me,
Grant me your gnosis, enlighten me.
At last the day dawns and truly I see
My home is not here but in eternity.

Clinton Cox

Coming Home

I've been away
Now I'm coming home
To the land of my birth
No more to roam
I think of the years
That we were away
Enjoying our lives
We wanted to stay
But now it is time
For me to come home
We were 'together'
Now I am alone
I think of the years
That have gone in between
The small cottage we shared
The valleys so green
The little Welsh chapel
Where we'd kneel and pray
And thank the good Lord
For each blessed day
My heart swells with pride
A tear dims my eye
As through the plane window
Green fields I espy
I build up a picture
In my mind's eye I see
The mist on the mountains
The swell of the sea
Now I no longer
Feel so alone
As I imagine Welsh voices
Calling me home
There's a little Welsh village
I long to see
Where I lived as a young man
It's called Abergele
My journey's nearly over
Now I can see
The white cliffs of Dover

Jutting out to the sea
Now I am nearing
The end of my quest
I'm coming home
To the land I love best
Wales Hiraeth

Margaret Toft
Abergele 2002

My Girls, My Dreams

'It's a girl,' cried the nurse, 'it's a girl, it's a girl!'
The pain, hard work now over, already forgotten,
'It's a girl,' I am told, floating, my mind in a whirl
With this new little life I was already besotten

She was handed to me all wrapped but her face
I just wanted the whole world to wait,
Life couldn't just continue at the usual pace
With this miracle now here, albeit somewhat late

I wanted time to admire this wondrous creation
No one had achieved this perfection to date
Before this miracle could be shared with the nation
I thought the world should stop, look and join in my state

A lifetime of hopes and dreams started here
That would never have been dreamt for myself
Love, happiness, health, increasing year on year
As well as all things good I added wealth

Two years on and once more gifted the same joys
With none of the feelings lessened or waned
More love, happiness hopes, dreams and of course toys
I could only watch,in wonder, at what my life had gained

Someday I will lose out to the world and to life
But for now I will cherish and pray
Should they ever encounter trouble or strife
God will be by their side, to show them the way.

Morag Grierson
Drafted- August 6th 2008

171

I'm An Old Blue Bike

I'm an old blue bike, I was once loved too,
like the one he's got now all shiny and new.
I may be quite old, but I'm still young at heart,
My only problem is my engine won't start.

My problem is major so he's left me to rust,
in a shed in the garden, where I'm covered in dust.
Oh! I've lost my attraction, it's clear to see,
I don't get the reaction once dear to *He*.

He is the bloke who paid for me first,
when of me he first spoke, he was near fit to burst.
'You should see my bike, it's the best on the street.'
No other biker could ever compete.

I was nursed never cursed, 'cos we were a team,
I was washed and then polished, till I shimmered and gleamed.
That's the treatment I had, each day of the year.
Me, be neglected? That was never a fear.

I took it for granted, we never would part,
It's a terrible let down when your engine won't start.

Avis Scott
1986

Polar Expedition

Polar island in the north,
surrounded by Arctic sea and fjords,
glazed in enormous cubes of ice,
frosty and blue as a winter's night.

Sailing into the upper fjord
the bay is frozen, we have to walk,
cross the ice by foot and sledge,
huskies pulling our food and tents.

Have to be cautious, we have been told,
the ice bear might be out for a stroll.

Crossing the island from south to north,
investigating, exploring, marking our posts.
Penguins become our best friends,
as we make our way through this no-man's land.

Our expedition will soon be over,
bringing back what we have discovered.
Turning my head as we set our sails,
I watch the island drift away.

Tove Selseth

Anchor Books Information

We hope you have enjoyed reading this
book - and that you will continue to enjoy it
in the coming years.

If you like reading and writing poetry drop
us a line, or give us a call, and we'll send
you a free information pack.

Alternatively if you would like to order further
copies of this book or any of our other titles,
then please give us a call or log onto our
website at www.forwardpress.co.uk

Anchor Books Information
Remus House
Coltsfoot Drive
Peterborough
PE2 9JX
(01733) 898104